THE ART OF READING PEOPLE

A PSYCHOLOGIST'S GUIDE TO LEARNING THE ART OF HOW TO ANALYZE PEOPLE THROUGH PSYCHOLOGICAL TECHNIQUES, BODY LANGUAGE, AND PERSONALITY TYPES

LIN PEN

CONTENTS

INTRODUCTION

Congratulations on purchasing *The Art of Reading People* and thank you for doing so.

The following chapters will discuss scientifically researched techniques and strategies for how to read people in a variety of settings and interactions. The art of reading is not a new phenomenon; it has been around for hundreds of years in the Western world, and the ancient art of Chinese face reading dates back as far as 5,000 years. With this knowledge, you know that the strategies and techniques in this book are part of an established and proven science, guaranteed to show you results, even in your first few days of practice.

So, what exactly does it mean to read a person? After all, we're familiar with reading books and texts, but how does one read something like a human face? Let's look at an example to illustrate.

Many people all over the world make a professional living out of playing poker. And that's all they do. They win enough to make a comfortable living and travel all over the world to compete in tournaments against some of the world's best poker players. If you don't know anything about poker, you might be thinking, but isn't poker and gambling just about luck? Well, a lot of it comes down to luck, but in poker, whether you win or lose has a lot to do with how well you can read your opponents.

Poker players often talk about other players having some sort of "tell." A tell is some kind of gesture or behavior which gives away that they have a good hand. These tells can be so minute as to be a slight wiggle of the eyebrow or minute movement at the corner of the mouth. These movements that are almost undetectable to most people are the things that professional poker players are tuned in to look for and notice. If you see a poker player waiting for another player to make a decision, that person may be waiting and staring at the other players for a few minutes. Sure, this may be partially an intimidation tactic, but they are also looking for tells or anything to inform the decision they are about to make.

When people refer to having a good "poker face," what they mean is that the person is really good at hiding any and all expression or gesture that might give away what they are thinking. And there is a reason this works so well when poker players learn how to notice subtle human behavior.

The truth is human beings communicate in a variety of different ways when they interact, but did you know that only a small fraction of human communication is accomplished through speech? And further, a human being's speech is one of the most unreliable ways to read a person and surmise what it is they are thinking. People often lie, manipulate, or skirt the truth in an effort to hide something or give an intended impression that may not be perfectly in line with who they really are.

We can apply this to many different settings. The woman at the bar who sits alone may have a million intentions and ideas in her mind. If you are a man who is interested in approaching her, how do you decide if that is what she wants? How do you approach in a way that communicates you are friendly and good-intentioned? It's all a part of reading people through proven techniques that begin way before the first words are spoken.

Let's look at an example of how a person might communicate with body language instead of words.

Going back to the poker example, let's say a group of amateurs are getting together for a weekly poker night in someone's basement. Five guys gather and set their beers next to their places, maybe a few of them are smoking...okay, so this is the stereotypical version, but you get the idea. One of them deals the cards for a round of Texas Hold'em. As all of the men in the circle get their cards, they do their best to hide their expressions. One of the men, Tom, gets a full house on the first deal and immediately and unconsciously grins a bit. He almost lets out a laugh, he is so pleasantly surprised, but he knows he must try to hide his joy from the others. He puts his hand to his mouth, as if to wipe away some perspiration, then returns his attention to the game and looks around at everyone else. The person to his left is deadpan, staring at his cards, but his right foot is bouncing up and down underneath the table so hard that the vibration can be felt throughout the table. The man next to him looks like he's almost asleep, his head is downturned, and his eyes stare at the space in front of him. Next to him, a man looks at Tom as he observes the gestures he's trying so desperately to hold in, smiles to himself, and then folds his cards. He's successfully read Tom, through his physical gestures, and makes the decision to fold his cards because whatever Tom has in his hand, it must be good!

All of this was surmised through careful observation without anyone saying a word. Once you've memorized some of the basics of reading body language, you can begin to test your new knowledge on both people you know and people you don't. It works universally.

We will also be discussing the aspects of the "Big 5" personality traits which are: Openness, conscientiousness, extraversion, agreeableness, and neuroticism. We will also touch on some of the more popular and widely known personality type assessments, such as the Meyers-Briggs test, but it is important to note that the Meyers-Briggs assessment and personality types first developed by psychologist Dr. Carl Jung are not based on scientific research so much as a personal philosophy of observation by the early 20th century psychologist. He made careful observations of the people he knew and aligned these observations with his own theory, and the result is that even today, in the late 20-teens, we have people dedicated to the idea that they fit firmly into a personality type like INFJ (introversion, intuition, feeling, and judgment). Though these are all certainly valid personality traits, the Meyers-Briggs is generally considered invalid among scientific and psychology professionals.

The Big 5 personality traits are gaining traction through widespread research as a broad and far-reaching categorization of human personality. Many individual researchers have demonstrated data-driven results in terms of the application of this theory in the human population. Ernest Tupes and Raymond Christal are responsible for moving forward with the first model which was introduced in the US Air Force Personnel Laboratory in the late 50s. A man by the name of J.M. Digman introduced his five-factor model of personality back in 1990, and it was further organized from there.

Applications

What exactly are the implications of being able to read people? Let's look at just a few of the wide variety of settings in which people may use the various techniques associated with cold reading, face reading, body language, conversation analysis, and personality analysis for their own personal intentions.

Most of the time, people embark on the quest of learning to read people because they want to learn how to influence people. That is their end goal. In a sales setting, for example, a salesperson who can successfully read, approach and influence a person is going to make a sale much more often than someone who simply applies the same standard script in the same prescribed way to any and every customer who walks in. There is a major difference, and the person who invests time and energy into gathering all the information about a person before trying to make a sale is always going to be more likely to succeed. As mentioned before, the majority of the work comes beforehand, reading people's body language and personality before even uttering a word to them.

How about the dating world? There is a whole science and world of research which focuses primarily on social attraction and relationships.

A young woman sits at the bar with a drink, and she appears to be alone. There are lots of different possibilities for why she is drinking alone. One of them, and the one some young man hopes is the true one, is that she is, in fact, waiting for Mr. Right to approach her and start a conversation. But how can he tell if this is his golden opportunity?

In general, a person's bodily orientation toward another person tells a lot about how that person feels about him.

So let's say the young man sits next to the lady at the bar and she seems amicable to his presence. Her shoulders are opened up in the direction of where he is sitting, even if only slightly, and her feet are slightly turned toward him as well. Her head is up and looking around, not buried with her nose in her phone or hanging down in front of her. This is another signal that she is open to talking. Now, it's the young man's turn. Women often "engineer" opportunities for men to approach them in settings like this where they are also looking to meet someone. But if no one takes the opportunities she broadcasts, the opportunity may be lost.

Our subject conjures up some confidence and turns to introduce himself. She gives him a smile and offers her hand. Bingo! He is off to a great start.

Finally, we can't talk about reading people without discussing the arena of criminal investigation and profiling. You've seen this kind of thing in TV shows and crime dramas. Now, of course, not all of these shows have it totally accurate. Sometimes it's just all about show and entertainment. So let's look at some ways in which officers and investigators can pinpoint someone who is lying and someone who is telling them the truth in an interrogation.

Again, these techniques are vastly more complex than we will be discussing in this book. Professionals will study and practice this skill for years before actively practicing in a professional setting, but you will get an introduction and some basic and very useful concepts and strategies right here in this book.

Crossed arms and a guarded expression usually means they are going to take some work to get to open up, but if the person is sitting without crossed arms and legs with their torsos oriented toward the interviewer, it is a good sign that the person is ready to talk a little more openly. Steady eye contact is also a good sign.

People often associate shifty eye contact or hidden eye contact with someone who is hiding something, and they are often right! Eye contact can also be used as a tool for gaining trust.

In each chapter of this book, we will look more deeply into each facet of reading people mentioned above, as well as analyze different settings and environments in which people may utilize these strategies. We will start by examining the implications of reading people and move on to the basics of personality types and the ideologies surrounding each. We will discuss cold reading and profiling methods in chapters 5 and 6, then move on to applying conversational phrases as a technique for probing and gaining information about a person's thoughts. We will examine how to reply in these situations, then discuss the philosophies surrounding human connectivity and how that plays into influencing people. Finally, we will discuss body language, cues and the art of redirection before closing with how you can continue to hone your skills and practice in the real world.

There are plenty of books on this subject on the market, thanks again for choosing this one! Every effort was made to ensure it is full of as much useful information as possible, please enjoy!

THE IMPORTANCE OF ANALYZING OTHERS INSTANTLY

In today's hyper-competitive modern world, there are many settings in which it becomes imperative to be able to read other people in your environment, at least at a rudimentary level. Just as with any skills associated with influencing the behaviors and opinions of others, there are those who use such skills for relatively benign purposes, like in a professional setting such as the sales floor, or in a criminal investigation, and there are those who use people-reading strategies as a way to manipulate or gain trust for not-so-benign purposes, such as cheating people out of their money.

Analyzing Others to Make a Sale

Earlier in the 20th century, during the heyday of scam artists such as fortune tellers and psychic mediums, many people fell victim to cold reading techniques in which the reader would convince people that they knew much more about them than the reader should know. This would lead to a sense of confidence and trust among potential victims, priming them for a performance that would ultimately lead to a hefty fee. Many of these scam artists were enormously successful before investigators and skeptical members of the public were able to debunk them.

Today, these techniques are used in sales settings as a way to gain people's trust by convincing them that the salesperson knows more about what they want than even the customer. Some of the pressure sales tactics that are used in some places are seen as unethical, and many salespeople walk a thin line between being good salespersons and practiced scam artists. At least some of the responsibility falls on people in the general public to be aware and alert when it comes to interacting with salespeople who seem a tad too earnest.

Let's focus at the moment on the salesperson who is just looking to make a sale on a door-to-door basis and who would like to use some reading strategies to help him make the sale. The difference between making a sale and failing to make a sale lies directly on the salesman's ability to read the potential customer or client.

When the customer opens the door, the salesperson is tasked with immediately presenting himself as open and honest. If a potential client senses that there is something not quite right about a salesman's approach or technique, it is usually an instant failure.

. . .

So our salesman, let's call him Stan, has a big smile and straight posture as the potential client opens the door. Stan earns a reciprocal smile from the client, and this is his first positive signal for the sale. He extends his hand for a handshake, and it is received. Stan is then invited inside. This represents a possible best-case scenario, but most of the time nowadays, when a person opens the door and finds a salesman, the response is not so warm. The salesman must work harder to gain the person's attention and trust, and there are many ways to keep a careful eye on the potential client to see whether or not he is proceeding successfully.

If the salesman is making his presentation and the client crosses his arms, this may be a signal that the potential client is on guard about the salesperson, as if getting ready to defend himself against any possible manipulation attempts. Because this can happen, it is an understandable fear. So let's imagine our salesperson picks up on this body language and makes an effort to make a personal connection with the potential client in order to foster a sense of connection and familiarity. He sees a picture of a famous speaker on the client's wall and makes a comment about how he is also a fan. The client may immediately drop the crossed arms and engage in a conversation about the speaker. This may seem like a deviation from the salesman's goal, but in fact, he has made a giant leap forward by helping the client to feel more comfortable in letting his guard down. There is now a connection between the two strangers that earns a small bit of trust, and the client is ready to continue the sales conversation. If the salesman continues talking with a smile and using body language tactics like moving the eyebrows and using friendly facial expressions, the potential client may mirror these actions, and this is a further sign that he is moving closer to a successful sale. We can apply the principles mentioned in the introduction regarding body posture and orientation to this potential client. If the torso and shoulder are oriented straight on toward the salesman, this is an excellent sign, especially if the feet are also pointed toward the salesman. This body language and posture suggest that the person is interested and listening to what the salesperson has to say. If the potential client is leaning against the doorframe facing to the side with feet pointed away from the salesman to the side, this is a signal that the person is just waiting for an out in order to end the conversation.

There is a lot to unpack in this example, but you should be able to see more clearly how much the most subtle gestures and behaviors can influence others and also broadcast signals to others about what people are feeling without expressing it verbally. The ability to analyze others instantly may offer benefits as subtle as being able to recognize an unethical salesman or as direly important as recognizing a dangerous person before they get too close. Let's look at some examples of both.

Analyzing People to Avoid Danger

Joe Navarro in his book *Dangerous Personalities* discusses four of the major personality disorders which plague modern culture and cause devastating emotional, financial, and psychic damage to victims. Over the past several decades, there have been numerous research studies and published findings in the realm of psychology surrounding dangerous personality types.

It is an ugly facet to the reality of human beings and human behavior, but there is a real and present danger associated with being influenced or manipulated by people with criminal or simply cruel intent. Many victims of narcissistic abuse by a loved one or partner end up feeling the effects and emotional damage long after the person has been removed from their lives. It is a sad reality, but there are ways to educate yourself so that you can be on the lookout for the warning signs that are often associated with these dangerous personality types.

The narcissistic personality is one of the most recognizable personality types and is characterized by an individual who holds the conviction that he or she is deserving of high regard and value above all others. He is the person who can do no wrong and will use others for his benefit, no matter the cost to the victim. The narcissist is often a compulsive liar and will manipulate others to gain their trust if he thinks he can get something out of the victim. He will also tend to neglect any feelings of guilt and is convinced that he is justified in doing whatever he can to control others and gain loyalty. The narcissist may go to great lengths with an ultimate goal of taking advantage of a trusting relationship, even putting on a face and demeanor opposite to his personality in order to gain trust and even love from the victim. This is what makes narcissistic personality so dangerous—they can often be very good at portraying a totally different persona to people in an effort to gain control and trust over time. It is a slow burn kind of strategy, and often their victims don't see it coming when the inner narcissist finally shows himself or herself.

. . .

An emotionally unstable person can also be a very painful experience for the person who is drawn in and becomes trapped by a sense of compassion and wanting to help the person. These unstable personality types often harbor deep-seated emotions or painful experiences that manifest in their relationships. Again, the victim may be unaware that someone is emotionally unstable until after a few weeks or months when people tend to be putting on their best face in a budding relationship. But the relationship may quickly devolve as the emotionally unstable partner drains the victim through a cycle of emotional episodes that seem endless. Arguments may go on far longer than is warranted with extremely elevated levels of emotion. The unstable person will tend to insulate himself or herself through playing the "victim" of every circumstance that causes them pain. They can also be very demanding in terms of time and energy, closing off their significant others to outside influence or support.

Another personality type that tends to cultivate a feeling of being a constant victim is someone who is paranoid. This is not to be confused with psychiatric conditions like paranoid schizophrenia, which is a far more clinical, severe, and medically diagnosable disease. The paranoid personality type is a person who is constantly seeing themselves as being hurt or mistreated in some way by others. They tend to hold grudges for long periods of time and tend to be very possessive in relationships, a lot like a narcissist. They may have very restrictive and unreasonable standards and constantly judge others for not meeting their standards of a good person. They are persistently afflicted with feelings of paranoia surrounding people in their environments, convinced that everyone is "out to get them." An important distinction between a paranoid personality and a paranoid schizophrenic is the absence of hallucinations, either internal or external.

Many of these character traits overlap between dangerous personality types. The final personality Navarro discusses is the predator. These people are out on the prowl, looking for people who may be easy to manipulate for their own gain. This personality is also quite arrogant and usually harbors a complex justification for why they can prey on others without feeling guilty or compassion. Many predators have had experiences with predators themselves or have come to hold a deep hatred for people in general based on prior mistreatment earlier in their lives. They may feel bitter about their life circumstances and have the view that they are being forced to do whatever they can to survive.

The human mind has an incredible capacity to justify our behaviors, especially when they are generally seen as unethical. "Well, hit my sister because she hit me first." "I have to steal that money because without it I can't send my kids to school." "People bullied me in high school, so they're responsible for turning me into this monster who wants to hurt people." The list is endless and as varied as the crimes committed by those who inhabit one of these and other dangerous personality types.

So, what can you do to avoid being a victim?

. . .

How to Recognize a Dangerous Personality

The specific techniques and strategies for reading people and avoiding dangerous personality types will be expanded upon as you go through this book, but in general, here are some important ways you can guard yourself against becoming a victim:

- *Trust your gut instincts*: If you have a bad feeling about someone, it may be your subconscious mind picking up signals that your conscious mind has missed. Trust it and move away.

- *Too much eye contact*: Positive eye contact can be a sign of friendliness, but if someone is making too much eye contact with you, he/she may be trying to read you or get something from you instead. If it feels creepy, remove yourself from the situation.

- *Smile that doesn't reach the eyes*: If a person seems odd or something about their facial expression doesn't seem right, look at their eyes. If a smile is genuine, you will see little crinkles at the outside corners of their eyes. A lot of fake smiling can mean they are trying to give you a false impression of themselves.

- *Notice and record patterns of deception*: If you catch the person lying, even about something trivial, consider whether or not this has happened before and start keeping track. A person who lies easily and often is never a sign of good nature.

- *Controlling behavior and emotional manipulation*: The best way to guard yourself against any dangerous personality type is to educate yourself on the tendencies and common characteristics. The more you know, the more you will be able to pick up on those traits when they are present in others.

- *Overly expressive*: This one is an easier one to look out for and notice. Oftentimes, people with dangerous personalities lack the self-awareness to be able to tell when they are overdoing it. If it looks and feels unnatural to you in your interaction with the person, get out of the situation. It will often feel like someone trying to sell you something, and the product is themselves and what they have to offer you, while they are actually focused on what they can get out of *you*.

These tips will form a strong starting point and foundation for learning to guard yourself against dangerous personalities. They also apply to other situations in which danger is present, such as someone who might try to rob you or manipulate you into giving them something before disappearing. Not everyone is willing to put in the time and effort of a relationship to get something they want from you. Store managers learn to recognize behaviors that may signal that a person is hiding something they've just stolen. Police officers learn how to tell when someone is lying or hiding something, tipping them off to the possibility that the person is hiding criminal action or possession.

In the next chapter, we will discuss the characteristic associated with the "big 5" personality types. We will also look at some additional dangerous personality disorders like the sociopath and psychopath, as well as a borderline personality disorder.

At this point, I want to emphasize that although it is important to be able to recognize and guard yourself against dangerous personalities, there are many areas of overlap in behavior between people with bad intentions and those who are just suffering from a mental disorder. Not everyone who is arrogant is also a psychopath, and not everyone who has anxiety is emotionally unstable and manipulative. Use your powers of judgment and instinct to help you distinguish between the two. Sometimes someone who asks for help from you really just wants or needs assistance. There are ways to offer assistance to strangers without putting yourself in danger.

TYPES AND IDENTIFICATION OF PERSONALITY

As briefly introduced in the introduction to this book, one of the most popular and widely recognizable forms of personality identification is the Meyers-Briggs personality test. It is popular and fun and aims to offer insight into a person's inner workings, but there is no hard data to support the validity of such a test.

In this chapter, we will focus on the "big 5" personality types as offered and built upon through data-driven research.

To review, the big 5 are: Openness, Conscientiousness, extraversion, agreeableness, and neuroticism.

Let's briefly discuss the identification of each.

Openness is a very broad domain which encompasses much more than simply being open to others. Someone who scores high in this area is very interested in learning all that they can from the world and the people in it and may have numerous and varied areas of personal interest or hobbies. The world can be a playful thing for this person, and in their minds, there is an endless array of possibilities waiting for them to explore. It is easy to associate a sense of almost childlike euphoria to the mindset of someone who is open like this, and it rings quite true. Instead of seeing themselves or their environments as limiting, they rather focus on the possibilities present through opportunities. Someone who is not open is more likely to miss out on opportunities because they do not have the perspective that they exist or are waiting for them to discover. This concept touches on the concepts and theories surrounding positive thinking and the so-called law of attraction. Because the open individual moves through life with a kind of open-arms attitude, they tend to "catch" more positive life experiences simply through virtue of being open to them.

Conscientiousness refers to the capacity and tendency to be hyper-organized and methodical. These people are rarely late to an important appointment because they've thoroughly planned their day and have prepared for multiple possibilities for how their days might be altered. You can count on someone who scores high in conscientiousness because they tend to have a high degree of integrity and sense of responsibility. They would not let down a friend if they can help it because it would reflect poorly on them. Conscientious people are more likely to slip into the area of perfectionism, where anything less than perfect is unacceptable. They are thorough in their work and tend to perform at a higher level of efficiency than their peers of lesser conscientiousness.

A more familiar term to most people, extraversion refers to how someone gets their energy in relationship to others. Extraverts tend to want to be around other people a lot more often than introverts because they thrive in that environment. Introverts need time to themselves to recharge after lots of social interaction. They often tire quickly from too much social interaction, while extraverts can party all night long. Again, these are broad categories, and maybe one day the research will begin to show an even greater detailed picture of how human beings break down within the category of extraversion. For example, many people demonstrate interesting hybrids where in certain situations and environments they feel like extraverts in that they crave attention and social interaction, and in other environments, they feel much shyer and feel the need to be by themselves after other personality types wear them out. This category also doesn't seem to take into account certain personality characteristics that are resultant of neurological differences, like autism.

Agreeableness is pretty much what it sounds like to you. Someone who scores high in agreeable is likely to exude kindness and warmth toward other people, even in stressful situations. They are approachable, friendly, and easy to talk to when you first meet them. They tend to adopt a lot of the more open body language signals, like big genuine smiles and standing or sitting without legs and arms crosses and bodies oriented toward the person or people they are interacting with.

Finally, neuroticism involves a degree of emotional instability. Those who score high in this category tend to experience a lot of emotion that changes and is often more negative than positive. Think of someone who tends to worry constantly, more so than what we would consider "normal." This is someone who worries not just occasionally about things like a loved one going on a trip or a big bill they haven't paid, but about mundane things on a daily basis. Some people who score high in this category may also experience more serious mood disorders, like bipolar disorder, in which moods swing from severely depressed to manic over the course of weeks and months. This category connects with one of the four dangerous personalities we discussed in the last chapter, the emotionally unstable personality. When someone uses other people for their own gain or their own comfort without regard to how it affects that person, then you have someone who is willing to completely drain another emotionally in order to alleviate symptoms of an emotionally unstable or high neurotic personality. Again, there are important differences that one must be able to recognize between someone who is suffering emotionally and is asking for help in an appropriate way and someone who is looking to manipulate and hurt that person.

What are some signs you can watch out for to determine where a person lies in terms of each personality category? Let's start with neuroticism and work our way back up with some key ways to discern personality type before even uttering a word to them.

Someone high in neuroticism will exhibit signs of emotional stress. This may look like fidgeting on some part of the body, like someone who bounces their leg up and down constantly during a meeting, or another nervous tendency like biting one's nails incessantly, even in public, crinkled forward like they are thinking hard, or a generally disheveled appearance on a regular basis. As always these are all simply signs that a person may be experiencing emotional stress, not a guarantee. The key is to observe the person over time. Everyone gets stressed out from time to time, but if someone demonstrates signs of emotional instability over the course of months or years, then there is a good chance that he/she is a naturally highly neurotic personality. Also, if it is someone whom you can observe at work or in school or some other setting, observe how they interact with others and how often. Are they constantly going up to others to tell them about their day or how they are suffering from this or that issue? Do they constantly need to share their nervous energy with others to feel better? These may be signs of an unstable personality, and the person may be trying to nurture the need to feel like a victim in all uncomfortable situations, even if they brought those circumstances on themselves.

Agreeableness is an easy one, though most people's personalities are a complex mixture of these categories. But someone who is high in agreeableness is going to show it on their faces, in their behavior, and in the ways, they interact with others—because they genuinely enjoy it and care for other people. These types are a treasure to have around you and in your life. Think of the teacher or store manager who seems happy and satisfied with their jobs and likes to encourage others around them. They may be more attuned to pick up signals from others because they are outwardly focused instead of inwardly focused, which may be a sign that they would score high in extraversion as well. Because they seem to have their own lives figured out, they don't spend all of their time in their heads worrying or thinking about themselves. These are the kinds of people who go on to get involved with charity organization or nonprofits looking to help those less fortunate in their communities or in communities around the world. They may be more capable of thinking on a larger scale and you may see them always talking openly and excitedly to others about their ideas and plans. They are also very good listeners. Instead of constantly thinking about what they want to say while you are talking, like perhaps someone who is much more emotionally unstable or predatory, they are intently listening to your words. They will make positive eye contact with you and stop what they are doing to listen to you. Agreeableness is a great personality type to have in your life.

Moving on to extraversion, let's picture a scene at a party where there are many young 20-something gathered for a get-together. When you look around, you see a lot of different things going on. Let's say there are a few people who seem to be like magnets, drawing people to them as they talk with big gestures and share amusing stories. She works to make eye contact with everyone around her and includes other people as she talks to solidify a kind of glue that keeps people listening to her. This may go on and on for hours, and she may rotate between groups of people, always maintaining a high level of energy. She never seems to tire of smiling.

In contrast, picture the guy who shows up a little late. He may be alone or with a few friends. He rotates with his friends but doesn't go out on his own or strike up conversations with people he doesn't know. He smiles when he is being interacted with but doesn't seem to maintain the energy to keep the smile on his face and consequently doesn't appear as if he is having a good time. These would all be signs of low extraversion or introversion. He may think of an excuse to leave a little early at the end of the night and doesn't necessarily take the time to say goodbye to everyone he's met that night.

Again, keep in mind that different personalities may behave differently in different settings, and you will always become more accurate about a personality type the longer you can observe a person, preferably in different settings. The same guy who seemed shy and introverted at the party may come alive in a work setting where he feels confident and energetic. He may love his work and love working with others toward a goal and simply feel out of place in a frivolous setting like a party with people he doesn't know well. Careful observations will continue to offer clues into the extent to which a person may be categorized as high or low extraversion. If he tends to have high energy at work but consistently turns down social invitations after work, then he may be low extraversion and simply strongly motivated by his work, which leads us to the final category.

Those who score high in the conscientiousness category will display lots of clues about their personality type. When you think of someone who is self-described as a perfectionist, what does this mean to you? You may imagine someone who is hyper-organized, always has work done on time that is impeccably complete. Their workspace is always clean and there is a place for everything that they use every single day. Their appearance will usually reflect their organization and attention to details. They will look essentially well "put together" and their interaction with others may be agreeable but a little forced due to their perception that they must never say anything "incorrect" or say the "perfect" thing to others to make sure their status and social connections stay strong. People high in conscientiousness may also carry around a great deal of stress because of their addiction to organization and pressure to be good at everything they do. They may be more likely to listen to you while shifting their eyes or fidgeting in some way, which suggests that they feel self-conscious and are doing their best to hide it. It is an interesting paradox that people who seem the most on top of things may secretly harbor a high degree of self-consciousness. This is because they find it very difficult to perceive themselves as good enough, always striving to be better and closer to a perfect vision of themselves in one aspect or another. Those high in conscientiousness may also overlap into an emotional instability or neurotic state if they begin to translate their perception of pressure to be perfect into constant or generalized anxiety. They may need constant reassurance that they are doing a good job and seek validation from others.

According to research, every human being's personality is a complex mesh of traits and characteristics, many of which fall into these broad categories. The ways in which people interact with each other often offer insight into their inner lives and feelings towards the people they interact with on a regular basis. If you are a good observer, you may be able to pick up on the signs and signals which can tell you whether or not a person is highly stressed out or neurotic, or if someone is a perfectionist and feels constant pressure at work or in school or as a partner, etc. A lot of this information can be gleaned from a simple conversation, and many people are open to direct questions, such as "Do you view yourself as an extravert?" In general, people like to talk about themselves. They like it when others want to talk about them, and many people will offer intimate information to the right people. The key to getting people to open up about themselves is to present yourself as a person whom they can trust. We will get into this in more detail in the following chapters.

Next, we will discuss the persona and how different personalities interact in an effort to gain trust and rapport for various intentions. We will also take a look at some of the characteristics of people who fall into the extreme personality types of a narcissist, borderline personality disorder, and the psychopath and sociopath. We will also discuss how people with dominant personality traits in each of the big 5 categories tend to interact with each other and how to discern whether someone is trying to manipulate you into giving them something they want. It is imperative to develop the awareness and skills to protect yourself from people who may have ill intentions. But it is also important to be open to helping others who genuinely need help, especially if they are people whom you love and trust.

INTERACTION STRUCTURE OF EACH PERSONA TYPE

So, LET'S START WITH MAKING AN IMPORTANT DISTINCTION between the words "personality" and "persona."

As we discussed in the last chapter, personality is a complex structure of traits and behaviors which make up a human being and how he/she interacts with the world and the people in it. Persona is what people project to others and is an effort to display exactly how they want to be seen by others. This persona may or may not align with their true personalities. Think of a professional magician. Let's call him Mr. Magic (original, right?). Mr. Magic likes to do street magic and is always costumed like an illusionist from the 20s in the US. His costume is consistent with the era, and he has practiced talking using vocabulary and figures of speech that were common during that time. Mr. Magic's real name is Sam, but he never gives his real name to people while he is working. Mr. Magic is Sam's *persona*. Mr. Magic's personality as he interacts with people may either be similar to his personality when he is not working or very different. But the key difference to recognize here is that the persona is a *construction.*

People use personas in everyday life, not necessarily as part of their professions. Teenagers often experiment with different personas as they find groups to try and identify with or if they decide they want to be seen as something that is different from who they really are. Someone who is self-conscious and easily intimidated may decide to dress like someone who is tough so that people might think twice about messing with him. On the outside, he looks like he runs with a crowd of "tough" people, but inwardly, he is terrified that someone will call his bluff.

Adopted personas are not always so extreme. A common persona adopted by many professionals all over the world is the persona that comes out when a businessperson or salesperson is talking to a potential client. Individuals in professions that deal with sales and talking to business-minded people often must adopt a persona that is conducive to winning over a client in the hopes of solidifying a contract or making a sale. This persona is usually not exactly aligned with the person's personality, but instead adjusted to fit a model of what a client will find attractive and trustworthy in terms of their money and feeling confident in a purchase. Many professionals in this arena practice something called "mirroring" when they interact with clients as a way to gain trust and instant rapport.

. . .

Mirroring Strategies for Gaining Trust and Rapport

Mirroring is a simple concept but takes some time and practice to develop the skill so that it comes off as natural and not fake.

Everyone does a bit of mirroring naturally to some degree when they interact with others, especially if they are meeting someone new and want to get on the person's good side. Let's illustrate by looking at an example.

Let's say you just got promoted at your job and you are a little intimidated. You've been working hard to show your boss just how amazing you are at your job and finally, after two years, your hard work has been rewarded. The promotion involves getting a whole new office and working under a new person to whom you will begin to report on a daily basis. Let's call this higher-up Bob.

The next morning, you are called in to meet your new boss, Bob. You walk in, and he is standing next to a large window which his arms linked behind him. His posture is straight as an arrow and as he turns around, you see that his face is quite expressionless.

. . .

You walk forward to extend a hand as you are introduced. He moves toward you to meet the gesture.

What you do not notice is that as soon as you evaluate your new boss and the details of his appearance, posture, and stance, you immediately begin to subconsciously adjust your own posture to mirror his. This is a subconscious attempt to form an immediate bond or feeling of familiarity with this person whom you are trying to impress. As you move your hand out to shake Bob's hand, you adjust the length of your stretch and even the pressure of your shake to mirror that of Bob's. If Bob makes small, stilted gestures, like tiny head bobs to signify confirmation of information as you speak, you also tend to make those same movements. Not everything you do perfectly mirrors Bob's behaviors, but a great many small things fall into place that way, and you may not even notice it happening.

Those who consciously mirror are tasked with making the mental effort of observing and mirroring but without making it obvious what they are doing. Different personality types will tend to have varying degrees of alertness when it comes to mirroring, so the practitioner must be careful about who he or she chooses to practice on! If someone picks up on the fact that you are consciously mirroring them, they may take it as a sign that you are manipulative or untrustworthy.

. . .

But what happens if you are successful? As mentioned in the previous chapter, people very much like to talk about themselves, whether they will admit to it or not. People also tend to like you more if you use their names in conversation regularly because they also like to hear their own names. It builds an unconscious, subtle sense of trust and affinity that becomes important as you combine this strategy with others to build rapport. Going back to the executive and his new boss Bob, making an effort to use Bob's name in conversation combined with subtle mirroring will go a long way in this initial interaction as they construct what their professional relationship will look like going forward.

Interaction Between Big 5 Personality Types

People interact with each other in an endless variety of ways, but there are some key differences to keep in mind when you decide to begin an interaction with someone dominant in one of the big 5 personality types.

Engaging with someone high in conscientiousness may take a bit of finesse simply because of the tendency toward being "high-strung." People high in conscientiousness are not necessarily overly perfectionist or weighed down by pressure they put on themselves, but when you decide to approach someone like this, it may be better to err on the side of caution.

. . .

Do not interrupt someone who is conscientious when they are busy working. Period. Especially if you just want to make a friendly introduction. They are likely to look at this as a very rude interruption and waste of their time when they have tasks they consider more important to do. These people are not the types who are constantly taking "breaks" from their work in order to talk and joke around with someone in the next cubicle. Wait for a time when they are more relaxed. Perhaps you wait until a Friday afternoon or when the workload in the office is a little lighter. Observe their facial expressions. If their foreheads are crinkled like they are concentrating on something, it is still not a good time to approach. It may be best to catch them during a lunch break or outside the office after they've left for the day.

These principles apply to many different settings where you find this personality type. The most important thing is to wait to talk to them until they are more relaxed, generally when they are not engaged in a task that they feel pressured to perform to the best of their ability. Other people at this point are just distractions.

The other tough personality to crack would be the highly neurotic. Time of approach is also very important here, as an ill-timed approach may just work to heighten levels of anxiety. When dealing with someone who tends toward neuroticism, there are body language techniques that may come in handy when you want to approach this person without appearing threatening.

. . .

Do not approach straight on. Orienting your shoulders, torso, and feet directly toward this person can feel very overbearing and intimidating. The person may even cower back from you. Instead, approach from the side and orient your body in the same way that their body is oriented. If they are walking down the sidewalk, approach at an angle and immediately turn so that you are walking side by side. Do not try to stop them and keep your tone of voice in mind. Do not speak too loudly and offer a kind greeting along with a smile and subtle eye contact. Your next step is to gauge how this person is reacting to your approach, and we will go into more detail in the chapter on cold reading, but the main idea is to not introduce additional sources of anxiety for the person who tends toward neuroticism.

The other personality types in the big 5 groupings, agreeableness, extraversion, and openness will naturally be easier to approach and interact with on a first-time basis. Keep in mind that human beings are unique and variable creatures. Just because someone may be tricky to interact with at first doesn't mean they won't become much easier to talk to as they get to know you. Everyone has a different experience with different types of people, and sometimes they need extra assurance that you are worth their time or are non-threatening to them.

Mirroring will be very successful when you decide to introduce yourself to someone who is high in agreeableness, extraversion and/or openness. Be sure to smile and orient yourself toward the person you are talking to in order to make it clear that you are interested in what they have to say and are not distracted. Remember to listen just as much or more than you are talking. Again, people love to talk about themselves and hear their names, so whether you are approaching for a romantic interest or trying to sell a new client on a product, remember to make them the center of the conversation and the center of the interaction.

Before moving on to extreme personality disorders, I want to discuss briefly how people should consider those suffering from mood disorders and how this should not always be looked upon as a predatory or manipulative mechanism. Bipolar disorder and borderline personality are clinically diagnosable and treatable mood disorders that need immediate attention. Neuroticism is different in that it is one facet of a personality which may manifest more strongly than others and is not a medically recognized mood disorder. Anxiety is often a component of neuroticism, and anxiety itself is a naturally occurring emotional phenomenon that manifests as a result of life events, but acute, long-term anxiety in the forms of social anxiety and generalized anxiety disorder are also psychologically recognized conditions which may require treatment such as therapy and medication.

A lot of misinformation and stigma remain in the orbit of a diagnosis of borderline personality disorder, but this condition should not automatically be associated with predatory and manipulative personality disorders like psychopathy, sociopaths, and narcissism. It is natural to want to categorize people and put them into boxes but remember that people are amazingly complicated creatures and that there is a fluidity present when it comes to identifying personality traits, behaviors and motivations. With this in mind, let's move on to narcissism, psychopathy and the sociopath.

The Narcissist, Psychopath, and Sociopath

It is impossible to discuss personality without also touching on the basics of what makes a true narcissist, psychopath, and sociopath.

These identities have long been an area of fascination for the general public and fans of true crime as they are often associated with some of the most widely known and infamous criminals in human history, such as Ted Bundy and Jim Jones.

Narcissism is characterized as a person who cares only for himself, deems himself better, smarter, more deserving, and deserving of respect above all others. He/she will manipulate and hurt others for his/her own gain without feelings of remorse and always harbors a personal sense of justification for his/her actions. The most dangerous thing about these personality types is that they are very good at pretending to be what they are not. Narcissists often invest weeks, months or even years into a relationship before making a move on what they want out of the partnership, whether it is money, control, or another thing of value.

. . .

Sociopaths also tend toward manipulation of others for self-gain and lack any sense of remorse or guilt about their actions. Narcissism, sociopaths, and psychopaths all have specific diagnostic criteria within the most recent edition of the DSM, or Diagnostic and Statistical Manual of Mental Disorders. Many of the characteristics underneath each of these three disorders overlap, but there are some key differences.

Psychopathy is essentially a more severe form of the sociopath and will manifest much more severe symptoms. The psychopath may also have a delusional sense of capability and take risks that others would deem insane as he is convinced that he can do many things that other mere mortals cannot. While many sociopath characteristics overlap into the psychopath category, a few key differences according to the DSM include that sociopaths must have demonstrated occurrences of reckless disregard for the safety of themselves and/or others, repeated law violations, and pervasive lying and deceitfulness. They may also be physically aggressive. The lack of empathy and guilt is less severe in a sociopath than a psychopath, and the sociopath may be able to form some kind of bond with others. Additionally, traits and behaviors in sociopaths associated with the condition have been shown to lessen as the sociopath gets older in some cases, while in almost every case, the psychopath does not undergo any kind of transformation as they grow older. They essentially have little to no hope of learning or developing a sense of empathy or guilts, making them what many call "lost causes" in human society.

THE IDEOLOGIES OF INSIGHTS

WHY DOES A PERSON OR ORGANIZATION DEEM IT NECESSARY to possess the skills of reading people to gather information on them? In this chapter, we will discuss a few of the different ideologies and postures associated with information gathering as well as the extreme forms associated with a severe preoccupation with "the other" like paranoia and phobias associated with people. We will first discuss the theory of mind as a starting point to the psychology that is involved when we talk about the natural human curiosity toward "knowing" the "other."

Theory of Mind

To briefly define the theory of mind, let's look at an example of how the theory of mind is present in children starting around age 6 but has been proven to be a learned skill because the theory of mind is absent in children around age 3.

. . .

Let's say we sit down with a young child who is 3 years old; let's call her

Cindy. We paint a scenario for her. In the scenario, an adult has a basket to her left and a box to her right. A young boy, Jimmy, approaches the adult who holds a small ball in her hand. Jimmy notices the ball and watches as the adult places the ball in the basket. Jimmy is taken out of the room and the adult takes the ball out of the box and places it into the box instead. Jimmy returns.

Now, we ask Cindy, aged 3, "where will Jimmy look for the ball?" At age 3, children will automatically point to the box because they know where the ball is and they do not have the insight yet that Jimmy has different knowledge in his mind. Jimmy will still look for the ball in the basket because that is where he saw it placed.

When the same study is conducted with slightly older children, around age 6, an interesting shift happens. Children this age are able to differentiate between what they know and what they think another person knows, and consequently how they will behave as a result of their own knowledge. This is called the theory of mind.

As we get older, the theory of mind plays a greater and greater roll in our lives. As teenagers, typical Americans are constantly preoccupied with how they are perceived by others. Remember the tough guy example from our discussion on a persona? Personas are often formed in an effort to influence what others think about us because, ultimately, without some kind of information gathering, *we just don't know what people think.* This is where the art of reading people comes in.

When we want to know more about a person than we currently do, on a one-to-one scale, a person must utilize a set of tools that have to do with observation in order to glean information on a short-term basis. But let's blow the idea of people reading and information gathering way up into a large-scale view. Many modern developed countries have a complex structure of organization, both open and covert, whose sole responsibility is to monitor other countries and persons of interest within an agreed upon set of parameters. The FBI and CIA are tasked, among many other responsibilities, to keep a constant, watchful eye on anything or anyone which may manifest as a source of national threat. Persons in the form of spies infiltrate other countries under the guise of an ambassador or another position with the goal of gathering information without anyone else knowing about it. At the top levels, these mechanisms are in place in order to detect threats before they have time to turn into reality. In America, the initiation of the PATRIOT Act followed soon after the events of 9/11 in order to better enable authorities and information-gathering organizations to identify and thwart terrorist efforts.

All of this is an example of the ideology of self-defense through information gathering. Knowledge is power, as they say. The more we know about a potential threat, the better we can deal with it as a country; this is the mindset that goes along with the ideology.

. . .

So the ideology works both on a large scale and on a small scale. Individuals go to great lengths to secure their homes to keep their families safe from potential intruders. They get concealed carry licenses so they have the sense of safety wherever they go, confident that they would be able to defend themselves in a bad situation.

But this is a reactionary approach. You're in a grocery store and you notice as you walk up to the front counter that someone has pulled out their own gun and is pointing it at the cashier and demanding money. What do you do? You have a gun in your purse, but to pull out your gun might scare the guy into shooting and running away. You don't want the situation to escalate. This is a poor reactionary position because you are surrounded by potential victims and anything you do to antagonize the robber may do more damage than a few stolen bills. You decide to lay low like everyone else and wait for the person to leave with his stolen cash.

An unfortunate ending to the story, but what would have happened if you'd tried to intervene? Perhaps the scene you dream about would manifest and after having drawn your weapon and yelling a bad-ass one-liner at the guy, he turns and drops his gun. Someone calls the police, and you are seen as the community hero who saved the day. This action would assume that the robber was going to be intimidated by you, a civilian, with your own gun. There is a very good chance that instead, you wind up dead in this scenario.

. . .

Let's look at another possibility. One where the store manager or yourself is empowered by the fact that you know how to spot potentially dangerous individuals and know what actions to take to avoid the situation getting to the dangerous point it did in the last scenario.

A man walks into the store in the evening wearing dark clothes and a hat that partially covers his face. He walks slowly and is spending more time looking at the store staff than anything he might wish to buy. You also notice a strange bulge in the back of his pants just below his shirt. You alert the store manager, and he brings him to the attention of the security guard who patrols the area outside while having his staff spread the world about keeping an eye on this individual. After alerting security outside, the manager approaches the man and offers to help him find something. He stutters, unsure of what to say. At the front counter, if he is trying to move forward with his plan, the manager might stand just to the side of the cashier in order to form more of a physical intimidation factor. This lowers the confidence that the robber will get away with his plan, and reluctantly buys a pack of gum, then leaves.

An escalated situation was avoided in this situation because someone was able to read the body language and interpret the appearance and strange behavior as suspicious. We will get a little more into the definition and practice of profiling in a later chapter, but the point I want to make here is that a bad situation was avoided because of a person's knowledge of how to spot the warning signs before it could escalate. This is the power of knowledge and proactive information gathering.

Reactionary stances are often held by people who simply do not have the experience to know when to be proactive, or worse, they assume a proactive stance in a situation that simply makes a bad situation worse. When an individual becomes fearful in a situation that is unclear to him or her, then poor decision-making may come into play. This is a dangerous situation, especially if there are deadly weapons involved.

Paranoia

Paranoia involves feelings of irrational fear in connection with the delusion that everyone or an individual is "out to get you" or hurt you. A person who is paranoid will feel this is absolute, irrefutable truth and may begin lashing out in irrational ways, either reacting emotionally or physically as a way to defend themselves. This, in a sense, is a perversion of the information-gathering defensive posture. The paranoid person has a set of false information on which to go on in his/her decision-making process. This can lead to a very dangerous situation when the person is confronted with another whom he/she perceives as wanting to cause harm.

The terms paranoia and paranoid are commonly used in conjunction with labeling people who are not necessarily medically diagnosed with the condition but rather hold irrational beliefs as a result of false information-gathering. The extreme form of false information is a delusion. Oftentimes a lack of adequate information can be even scarier than false information because false information gives the person a grip on themselves regarding a starting point from which they can defend themselves. The human brain is constantly looking to connect the dots in what it is processing. When there is missing information, the brain will complete what is missing and fill in the holes based on prior experienced and based on the information that it already has. The trouble is, this process is not always empirically accurate. The brain may jump to conclusions based on false information, leading to a sense of danger and paranoia where there is, in fact, no threat. Think of someone stumbling around in the dark in an unfamiliar environment. The lack of information may lead the person to fill in the gaps with unpleasant assumptions about people or creatures waiting to pounce on them in the dark. This could be a harmless, playful phenomenon that a person quickly recognizes as their brains "playing tricks" on them, or it may manifest as a delusional belief that this gap-filling by their brains actually resembles reality. In extreme situations, delusions may turn into hallucinations, and this is where psychological diagnosis and mental illness comes into the picture. Children playing in the dark and tapping each other on the shoulder is a fun game of scaring each other than laughing as the child realizes it is only his friend in the dark. When fear becomes a delusion based on no information or false information, then we have a genuine fight or flight response to a threat that does not actually exist.

Another resulting condition of this lack of information or faulty information is anxiety.

. . .

Anxiety

Similar to fear and paranoia, anxiety is a common, natural experience in human beings that, if taken to the extreme, can manifest as a clinical mental disorder. Anxiety can feel like an onslaught of false information that plays like a broken record inside one's mind. As the brain moves to fill in the details where there is missing information, it is influenced by the emotional reactions and addictions that influence how you perceive and process other people and their behaviors. This can become a vicious cycle if it is not addressed properly, and many people continue to live with chronic anxiety for their entire lives.

Let's look at an example of how anxiety can alter one's perception of the people around her.

A woman suffers from anxiety. Her mother was the same way, and her mother before her. She has experienced violent behavior in the past by her father, whom her mother left when she was very young. Her father was a tall Hispanic man with a deep, baritone voice. As a result, whenever this woman is out in public and she sees someone who, in her mind, resembles her father, she starts to feel acute anxiety that borders on a panic attack. Her brain is trying to do her a favor by giving her information that a similar threat to the one that had once existed in her life is here again, and she should defend herself. Her brain is giving her false information based on prior experience. She does not, in fact, no anything about this stranger who happens to be tall and Hispanic.

. . .

On a large scale, we can look at the propensity for many people in rural white areas in America to harbor fear and even racist hatred for the minority communities in and around their towns and cities. Unfortunately, racism is handed down from generation to generation in areas where the history of racism runs deep and there has been no catalyst for a change in thought pattern. Children are taught to hate certain people by their parents at a young age, and many times, without outside influence or knowledge of their flawed perspective, there is nothing to challenge this insight of theirs to which they cling for the duration of their lives. With the influence of group mentality, the ideology is made even stronger because it is supported by lots of people instead of just a few, which is seen as a viable establishment supported by knowledge and perceived truths. It is human nature to seek status within their social groups, and if a person is born into an environment which cultivates racism, then this becomes a point of value within their own consciousness as a way to climb the ladder and be accepted as a valued member of the group.

Knowledge Is Power

What hope is there for a young person who is born into a community of people filled with hatred? Or for someone who is anxious about the "other"? How about a person whose fears build upon each other until there is a state of paranoia?

Knowledge is key to understanding and alleviating the emotionally detrimental reactions to the unknown. Introduce a person to someone who is characterized as other, and there may form a new understanding that instantly eliminates all of the false information that had once dominated that space in the brain. This applies not only to extreme situations of defensive ideology based on fear but also in small-scale, person-to-person interactions.

In order to set yourself firmly in a proactive, knowledge-based defensive posture for information gathering, you will need the tools to begin automatically deducing information about your surroundings and the people around. These tools will help replace any tendency toward false assumptions based on biased misinformation, bigoted misinformation or fear by focusing on immediate, empirical, observable data. In the next chapter, you'll learn about the fascinating world of cold reading.

APPROACHES FOR COLD READING PEOPLE

Cold reading has been around for thousands of years and connotes various strategies and styles whose ultimate aim is to create the belief in another person that you know more about him/her than that person knows about him/herself. The art of cold reading is associated with various forms of psychic reading.

The gist of the cold reading technique is to take someone whom you do not know and gradually convince this person that you know all about them. This can be done is as little as a few seconds or for longer periods of time. The cold reading may be a one-way series of statements towards the customer or it could be a longer appointment containing a back-and-forth dialogue that may or may not involve a series of corresponding actions. Let's look at a few examples which will probably sound familiar to you.

Psychic Readings and the Séance

One of the most popular subjects for modern horror films is the setting of the séance. In many films, the plot exposes the psychic individual as a fraud, but then introduces an unexpected entity that not even the psychic was expecting.

This scenario goes back a long way, and there is an almost romantic nostalgia surrounding the era of the early 20th century when psychic readers and the séance were quite popular as a way for people to contact their loved ones after death. Harry Houdini was known to hold a fascination with the afterlife and was convinced that he may be able to find a way to come back after death. After he lost his life tragically while performing one of his famous escapes, his wife pursued contact with him through an exhaustive parade of psychic readers and séances. Ironically, Houdini became famous during the latter part of his career for debunking "fake" psychics who were taking people's money and then essentially performing magic tricks during their séances to convince them that they were contacting the dead. Of course, Houdini recognized these tricks immediately.

His wife tried for ten years after Harry Houdini's death to contact him through a legitimate séance. They'd even agreed on a coded message which Houdini would use should he find a way to contact her from the afterlife. Bess was unsuccessful.

Radio shows in the later 20th century would periodically interview psychics and let callers call in to get their own brief reading. The psychics might bring in a set of tarot cards and proceed to give readings to many callers one after the other.

Those who called in were regularly convinced that they had communicated with a real psychic and had been given a little bit of insight into their lives and what they could expect in the near future.

So, what happens in a cold reading that is convincing? Let's dig into some technique.

First of all, people must realize that even though we are all different and unique in various ways, we are all human beings. We evolved to form similar brains which are connected to the earliest level of evolution that gives us the "instinct" to behave in conjunction with what is necessary for survival: We hunt and kill for food, we run away from danger, we find mates and form attachments and nurture our young, we naturally form groups in the form of the family or tribe or community, etc. But our brains have evolved further to form the highest level of brain complexity on earth. We are intelligent human beings with emotions and powers of reasoning, along with a perception of will. It is the personal thoughts, feelings, desires, ambitions, passions, etc., which convince us that we have unique lives with unique emotional experiences which cannot be exactly emulated by anyone else. The idea of the unique individual is further cultivated in modern Western society, which might be why the professional field of the psychic reader became so lucrative in Britain and the US.

To go back to a concept we discussed in chapter 3, people love to hear their names and to talk about themselves when they are interacting with other people. Status is an evolutionary need and is connected to survival in that we, as a species, will naturally gravitate toward and protect those of high social status. When an individual goes to see a psychic reader, and especially if they are paying a hefty fee to see a psychic reader, there is an intention and a need there. Another fundamental human truth is that people tend to hear what they want to hear and ignore the things that don't align with it. If you've ever read your horoscope just for fun online, you might gravitate toward the one or two things that sound attractive or accurate and pretty much ignore the rest, rationalizing that it can't be 100% perfect, but 60 to 80% is pretty good!

Psychic readers, especially in a one-on-one, in-person format, work on the principles of positive feedback. The reader will begin with general statements about his/her life which would apply to a vast majority of people in the society or culture the person belongs to. "You've gone through a very touch event in your life recently." Let's break this sentence down.

First of all, can you think of a single person you know who has not gone through some degree of an emotional challenge recently? The word recently is incredibly broad and will mean different things to different people. That's because the word becomes redefined based on the event that the reader is conjuring in the person's mind. Let's say the person happened to have lost an aunt of uncle two years ago. Well, relative to the person's life, two years ago definitely falls into the category of "recently," and so the person feels as though the reader has tapped into their personal life through psychic ability. If the reader can "hook" the customer early on in this generalized phase, the person will only become more and more convinced as the reading progresses. This is because he/she now has a foothold to begin gathering feedback from the person through body language and verbal responses which will essentially lead the reader toward truths in the person's life.

The reader may present one or several generalized statements based on the customer's reaction and confirmations. The reader looks for head nodding and smiles and other signs that the reader is on the right track, then follow those tracks further. Perhaps after this first general statement, the customer comments, "yes, I lost my uncle two years ago." The reader may then follow this line briefly before turning to the next topic. The reader may describe a typical grieving process and express his condolences, and the customer feels as though there is a real connection being made between herself and the reader.

The generalized statements often involve things like experiencing a lot of stress "lately," having money issues "recently," having some kind of romantic involvement that was unexpected, etc. As the reader watches the customer's reactions, the reader will follow and keep moving until the reader finds a foothold. Perhaps when the reader mentions a recent love interest, the customer smiles, and giggles. This is a lot like the "tell" we talked about in the example of playing poker in the introduction. The reader now has a direction to go in, and he can also introduce "predictions" which correspond with what the person wants to hear. "This romantic connection is going to develop." Well, of course, it is! One or the other!

Predicting one's future is much easier because the reader is simply tasked with finding a snippet of the customer's life that he/she is invested in, then elaborating on where the customer is going with it. Happy customers are paying customers, and the reader knows that the customer will be happier if they leave with some positive news about their future. Though the reader may also make it more interesting by throwing in that they should "look out for a challenge in the coming weeks." The word challenge could refer to absolutely anything, the no doubt, the customer will be able to apply this to their life as we all face challenges every single day of some variance and degree.

Let's move on to examine the psychic who claims to be able to connect with people's loved ones. The psychic reading of this type may occur in an open forum with lots of people sitting in front of the reader in a performance setting, or it may occur in a small room set aside for performing séances.

In an open forum, the reader may start by calling out a common name to the audience or to an individual volunteer. The name is always a somewhat common name. In America, the name might be John or Carol or David. The customer then confirms that he/she knows someone with that name. The reader may then ask if this person is living or dead. If the person is living, the reader might say something like, "I see, well I have someone on the other side who wishes to communicate something to John." If the person is dead, the reader may ask a few more questions to determine how close the customer is with the one who has passed, then say that John would like to communicate something to her. If it is a close family member or a close friend, the communication will be something more intimate, like "I love you," or "I miss you. Don't be sad." Again, especially when dealing with feelings of grief and sadness, a person is going to be much more vulnerable and receptive to comfort and support, ignoring the signs of fraud or trickery.

In Houdini's lifetime, the séance was indeed a theatrical performance which worked to make this kind of reading and connection with dead loved ones much more convincing. By introducing physical elements, like objects levitating on their own or sounds coming from above their heads and various other "psychic phenomena," the reader was able to convince the customer even more of their abilities. The customers would leave with a solid belief that they had made contact with their dead wife or husband not only because the reader was able to pinpoint the name and some details about the person's life, but because they had actually seen physical proof of the ghost's presence. Many séance practitioners would take the deception as far as possible by having assistants collect information on the customers beforehand for the psychic reader to use during the séance.

Modern Applications

In modern times, people have become much more skeptical in general, and only those who truly want to believe in psychic phenomena and things like communicating with the dead through séance do. But cold reading may be used as part of modern-day deception techniques in varying degrees.

Take the salesman who approaches a customer in his appliance store. He makes a general statement like, "You look like you came in because you need to replace something in your home." The customer may say something like, "Why yes, my toaster hasn't been working for a week." The salesman responds, "That is so fortunate! It just so happens we have these brand-new toasters on sale, but just for today!" The trained salesman can detect many things about a person based on their demeanor, body language, and reactions to general statements. She will adjust her sales pitch depending on factors she sees in the customer like urgency, friendliness, and whether the customer's stance is relaxed or tense. A customer who is tense and standoffish may need a little more encouragement before trusting the salesman. This is where things like smiling and eye contact and positive facial expressions as well as non-intimidating postures come into play. It is also helpful to be able to relate and/or commiserate with the customer to strengthen this perception of a personal connection. For example, the customer may be upset because her fridge stopped working and she needs a replacement immediately. The salesman might reply, "Oh no! I know exactly how you feel. That happened to me just a few months ago." Introducing similarities between yourself and the customer will help build rapport and start forming a feeling of trust. But it all starts with that cold reading and getting the customer to buy in.

Now, using techniques like these as a salesman is not necessarily grounded in deception. But self-proclaimed scam artists are notorious for utilizing a cold reading to gain people's trust with the intention of cheating them out of money or taking money under false pretenses. Scam artists often use other deception techniques in conjunction with cold reading to steal people blind right in front of them. You may have seen this demonstrated in an entertainment context where a professional magician invites people on stage or approaches people on the street to demonstrate. They engage in a generalized conversation until the magician hits on something that is personal to the volunteer. As they are momentarily distracted by this personal connection, the magician is free to use techniques like sleight-of-hand and misdirection to slip the volunteer's wallet or some other item right out of his/her pocket. The best of these professional magicians can steal something right in front of the volunteer's eyes without them noticing in a performance that perfects all of these elements with good timing.

As mentioned before, the power of influence, whether in the context of cold reading, positions of leadership, dating, or manipulation, lies in the power of knowledge. When you learn to glean small details from a person and how to use them to your advantage, you can gain a person's trust in a matter of seconds. In the next chapter, we will discuss the principles of profiling and how it used professionally and nonprofessionally. We will also discuss the tendency toward racial profiling and how this relates to group psychology. Criminal profiling can be a useful tool in the criminal investigation arena but can also easily be abused and used as a tool for racism and implanting false assumptions based in that fear of the "other" we talked about earlier.

USING PROFILING METHODS TO EVALUATE PERSONS OF INTEREST

Profiling methods are used most famously in the criminal investigation arena, where professional profilers take all of the information they have about a given crime and come up with their best guesses regarding the traits and characteristics of the offender or offenders. To demonstrate, let's look at a case of from back in 2002 which involved the murder of victims in the areas of Maryland, Virginia and Washington D.C. in the U.S. These crimes documented the actions of those who were later known as the Washington snipers.

In October of 2002, 10 people were murdered and another 3 injured within this area. What made this case difficult was that there were no apparent connections between the victims themselves. The victims were killed in various settings while engaging in different activities, and the authorities in charge of investigating the murders could not find rhyme or reason to connect them. Drawing conclusions and finding connections between victims is important in a criminal investigation because it gives important clues about the offender. If you have a group of victims who are all similar in that they are women with blond hair around the age of 20, then you have some important information about the offender. In one of the most famous serial killer cases of all time, Ted Bundy creatively used his charm and manipulative skills to lure young women to their deaths. Bundy's victims spanned geographically across a wide swath of the northeastern US and eventually in Florida. But the similarities in modus operandi and victim characteristics made it clear that the same perpetrator was responsible for all of these killings. Modus operandi refers to the way the murders were executed. Bundy's murder victims were most often bashed over the head and showed signs of rape and/or other sexual mutilation. Further, the victims tended to be young, attractive women with a hairstyle that parted down the middle. All of these details, in addition to the physical evidence, helped investigators to draw a picture of what their perpetrator was like. The individual was deemed a psychopath and obviously had no problem sating his desires by conducting these murders as often as he could be successful.

So, let's go back to the Washington sniper case. Unlike the Ted Bundy case, the victims in the Washington snipers case did not seem to have any obvious connection other than general proximity and the way in which they died. Each victim was killed from a distance with a single rifle shot. Professionals from all fields of law enforcement were brought forward to give their professional opinions and advice and profilers gave their efforts at drawing a picture of the offender or offenders as best they could devise. Many different professional profilers from the FBI and others who were self-taught came up with their own ideas, and it turned out that pretty much all of these profilers were off the mark when the snipers were eventually discovered. Some of the various profile characteristics offered up by professionals included that the person was probably a white man and into action movies with people like Arnold Schwarzenegger in them. Other profilers suggested there were multiple snipers, likely white males, who worked in a position where they got to exercise some degree of power over others, perhaps "construction" or maybe a "fireman."

The two perpetrators ended up being two black males who were unemployed war veterans.

You may be gathering at this point that criminal profiling is not an exact science, and you are right. Profiling is never the primary tool for criminal investigation, but rather a supplement to an investigation where there is not a lot to go on in areas that are usually depended upon for solving a case. Profiling is most often used in serious crimes, such as murders, and in serial crimes, like in the Ted Bundy case. Profiling was used alongside other investigative techniques to home in on the details of this person committing some of the most atrocious murders in human history.

The Criminal Investigative Analysis was developed after investigators behave noticing that perpetrators who had been caught and arrested for particular crimes showed certain patterns of behavior and characteristics in common with each other at their crime scenes. This proved useful and efficient, as they could narrow their investigations down to a pool of people who shared those patterns of criminal behavior at the crime scene rather than having to start with a very large pool of suspects, then narrowing gradually from there.

The idea is to look at a crime scene in detail to come up with possible details about who the perpetrator is. Let's stick with murder as our example.

There are many aspects of a crime scene which may give valuable clue about a person's identity, personality, even going into further detail like race, gender, and socioeconomic status. Aspects like location and environment in the area immediately surrounding the crime scene are important as well.

As an example, let's take two categories with a defined set of characteristics associated with them—the organized and the disorganized perpetrator, or in this case, murderer.

After examining the crime scene, does it seem like the crime happened suddenly without any planning at all? Or is there evidence that the crime was meticulously planned beforehand? Is the crime scene a mess with the weapon used still lying on the floor? Or is the place almost completely clean with nothing left at the scene? The answers to these questions may offer valuable insight as investigators try to paint a picture of who the perpetrator is and what he/she/they are like. Someone who falls more into the organized category is more likely to show a higher level of intelligence and social capability. He/she may also be of a higher socioeconomic status whose affinity for organization carries over into his/her professional and personal life.

Another important factor that comes into play when profiling is discovering the modus operandi and motive. As defined earlier, the modus operandi refers to how the crime is committed. When an investigator discovers multiple crime scenes where the victim or victims were killed in the exact same way, then an important link can be made, and the profiler can use this information to continue filling in the gaps of who the murderer is. A person who commits their murders in the exact same way and executes them without forethought and planning, removing as much evidence as possible from the crime scene, sounds like a pretty organized killer.

The motive is all about why a specific crime is committed, and if this information can be confirmed, it can be a huge leap forward for the profiler and criminal investigators.

Let's imagine a crime scene where a murder happens late at night in a person's home. The scene is a mess, though it seems the murderer made the decision to keep the murder weapon with him when he/she/they left. There is a safe open in the bedroom with missing cash, and it looks like the perpetrator/s knew exactly how to open the safe, as there are no signs of someone having to physically break into it. The area around the murder victim is filled with broken items, and there are signs of struggle on the body. What does this suggest to the criminal profiler?

Well, one possible assumption is that the prime motive is safe and stealing cash. Seeing as the safe seemed to be easily gotten in to but left out in the middle of the floor, it may be that there was some planning that had gone into the crime beforehand. The perpetrator knew that there was a certain kind of safe in the bedroom and that he/she would need to know how to open it. This suggests that the perpetrator may have to know the victim to some degree, or else had some kind of connection to him. The chaotic scene immediately surrounding the victim suggests that though the theft may have been meticulously planned, the murder itself was not. Perhaps the homeowner came home earlier than expected and the robbers were startled. The homeowner tried to fight the perpetrator/s in his home and the struggle ended up in a murder. The robbers then fled with the cash in a panic, but with enough wherewithals to not leave the murder weapon.

In this situation, you have elements of an organized killer or killers along with disorganized elements associated with a possible unplanned murder. This would suggest that the primary motive was robbing the safe, and not targeted murder.

These examples are meant to demonstrate how profiling is utilized in a criminal investigation. I am not a criminal investigator, of course, but hopefully, you understand a bit better just what profiling entails in the criminal investigation sector. Let's look at one more example.

A murder takes place inside of a dance club that is marketed toward single gay women. The club is located in a part of town that is associated with people of a higher socioeconomic status, and the murder takes place upstairs in the club reserved for VIP members. The scene is chaotic and there is a great deal of forensic evidence to collect. The murderer seemed to have dropped the murder weapon a short distance away from the club in an alley, along with a few pieces of very expensive jewelry.

Because of the area, the clientele, and the physical evidence, a profile begins to present itself in just the first few hours of the investigation. About 92% of the people who come into the club are white females between the ages of 21 and 35. The drinks are priced quite high, and the VIP club is reserved for members who pay high fees for private space within the club. Because the murder took place in one of these upstairs areas, investigators have some good clues about the murderer's sex and socioeconomic status. They also can deduce that, because of the chaotic scene, the murder may have been completely unplanned and the result of a sudden conflict.

In both of these examples, investigators used evidence and all of the details of a crime scene in order to create a possible profile of the perpetrators involved in the murders. It is important to note that the profiling occurs out of a knowledge base offered by the crime scene and is not based on prior assumption or bias. As part of a chapter on profiling, we should discuss racial profiling and how this tendency leads to false accusations and a pervasive assumption of irrational fear surrounding an individual race.

Racial Profiling

Racial profiling is defined as when someone uses race or ethnicity as the prime basis for suspecting someone of having committed a crime. As an example, a store manager follows around anyone who looks African-American and enters his store because of a preconceived notion that African-Americans are likely to steal from him. He's decided even before a crime is committed that this type of person is likely to commit a specific crime. Note that in a criminal investigation, profiling is used as a tool based on the evidence of a specific crime scene or characteristics of a crime based on the behavior and characteristics of previously convicted perpetrators. Racial profiling is an illegal and discriminatory practice that may be practiced consciously or unconsciously due to the influence of society or authority figures on those who are uninformed or misinformed. This circles back to the ideology of information-gathering that is perverted based on the influence of fear, misinformation, and bigotry.

One of the most widely known examples of racial profiling in the U.S. occurred en masse following the 9/11 terrorist attack on the world trade center in New York City. Because of this pervasive fear echoing throughout the nation, the response of many individuals was to automatically associate anyone who looked like they might be Muslim with the terrorists of 9/11. Muslim individuals or just people who appeared to others in the U.S. like they might be Muslim were disproportionately monitored, frisked at airports and various security checkpoints, and even escorted off planes without any basis other than how they looked.

The rampant cycling of misinformation and fear supported by skewed media reports and societal biases continues to influence how law enforcement is carried out in the modern world. Law enforcement officials are not immune to the influence of things like societal and community bias, peer pressure, and authority figures. When fear and misinformation take the place of a rational, data-based criminal investigation, what you get is a vastly disproportionate ratio of white versus black and Hispanic incarcerated individuals relative to the general population. Many efforts have been put forward to curb this tendency, but the problem continues on and unfortunately will continue as long as fear and anxiety are filling in the gaps where knowledge and understanding are missing.

Proactive, defensive structures based in knowledge, experience, and data-driven research will always pave the way toward accurate and ethical law enforcement practices and communities that are free of the misinformed fear surrounding the "other," in whatever form that takes.

In conclusion, before moving on to verbal examination and analyzing strategies, profiling in the criminal investigation context is a tool used in specific circumstances and criminal situations as a supplement to the investigation. It is founded in empirical data discovered and analyzed at the crime scene and surrounding areas and is very different from the commonly known concept of profiling in the context of predetermining guilt based on things like race, gender, ethnicity, sex, etc. Racial profiling, in particular, is a common example of how fear and misinformation influences our human tendency to protect against the "other" who is different in some way from ourselves. Associating crime with a particular race is never correct or ethical, and it is in society's best interest that we continue to move forward and make strong efforts to properly train and monitor law enforcement so that abuse of authority does not affect innocent people's lives.

APPLYING PHRASES IN CONVERSATION TO EXAMINE PEOPLE

When you first meet a new person, how do you behave and what do you say? Do you follow a similar script each time you meet someone new, or is the interaction based on your intentions? Of course, our behavior changes depending on the context of the meeting. It takes some degree of social skill to discern how to properly interact with someone on a date versus a job interview, for example.

There are different levels of formality that most people automatically adapt based on the situation and social expectations based on "how it's always been done." For example, the job interview.

When someone prepares for a job interview, he/she may feel a bit nervous about the situation, especially if it is a job that is very important to them. It may be some kind of evaluation for a promotion or a completely new career change for this person. Either way, it's a big deal. Let's call her Shaina. How does Shaina prepare?

Social expectations tell us that Shaina should look professional and put together in order to make the best impression with the interviewer. She should be clean, well dressed, and appear confident.

Shaina drives to the office where she will be interviewed, careful to be a few minutes early, at the least. When she walks in, she is greeted by a friendly secretary who shows her to a room down a long hallway where her potential boss is waiting for her. Her initial approach and interaction are very important.

How does Shaina control her first impression on her boss? Let's assume she does the majority of things correctly to build rapport with her boss. She walks in with good posture and a genuine smile, extends her hand as she introduces herself and offers a handshake, then follows the boss's direction to sit in the chair across from him. She keeps up her smile and attempts to answer each and every question thoroughly while keeping good eye contact.

Her interviewer offers questions such as, "Why do you want this job?" "What are your strengths and weaknesses?" "Why should we hire you instead of anyone else applying?" "Why are you leaving your previous job?" "What are your goals, and where do you see yourself in five years?"

The interviewers will typically be looking for certain elements in different answers, but generally, the questions are very open and leave lots of room for Shina to be creative and to impress her potential boss. "Why do you want this job?" is a very common question and helps the interviewer to gauge just how much the person really wants the job. Sometimes, people go after jobs simply because they need a job immediately and not because they are invested and aligned with the company's goals. Many interviewers in various companies are going to want to see a demonstrated interest in the specific company, not just in getting a job anywhere. This question will tell them what they need to know and may prompt some interesting nonverbal and subconscious behaviors and signals as well.

When someone is working hard to think of a good answer rather than answering naturally with an interest and/or knowledge that is already there, he/she will look like they are working especially hard to find the "right" answer through fidgeting, shifting eyes down and to the sides as they think, and his/her expression might momentarily move from attentive and pleasant to contemplative and stressed. If someone answers a question like this quickly, enthusiastically with an unchanged expression, it usually means that they are genuinely interested in the topic and answering honestly. Oftentimes, people simply think too hard when it comes to answering questions like this in a stressful situation. Instead of getting too worked up about an interview, it is best to relax and just be honest. A good interviewer will be able to see through anything else.

Another very common and probing question is, "What are your strengths and weaknesses?" Why would the interviewer want to know about strengths and weaknesses? Because this is a commonly used strategy for probing the job applicant's personality and character traits. Not only will the interviewer discover some simple data about his/her strengths and weaknesses, but the interviewer will also discover a lot about what the applicant thinks about him/herself in the process. If an applicant answers confidently with a well thought out response, then he displays a high level of self-confidence, which is usually a valuable trait in an employee. However, if he is unable to adequately answer the weaknesses part of the question, then it may show that he doesn't actually know that much about himself, only seeing his strengths. Perhaps he has a tendency to see flaws in others but not himself and tends to blame others for his own mistakes. This would not be a valuable trait to have in a new employee.

All of these questions have a common aim, and that is to try and glean as much information about a person as possible within a limited amount of time in order to make a decision about how well the applicant would fit in and perform in the open position. Skills and experience are important, but a person must also have the interpersonal skills to work with coworkers or communicate with potential clients, etc. Someone who believes herself to be smarter or more competent than everyone else would quickly earn a level of general unlikability in the office, which may hurt productivity over the long-term. Specific personalities may not be quite as important as long as the applicant is very skilled and displays at least a moderate level of social skill, but what if we're talking about a very different arena in which personality is nearly the most important factor in the interaction? Let's talk about the dating game.

Probing Someone of Romantic Interest

Most of us have probably been in a similar situation to the following: You are getting ready to go on a date with someone whom you've met recently. (Let's pretend you are a woman interested in a man.) You bought a special outfit just for this dinner where he says they dress nice. He is picking you up from your apartment soon, and you are making last-minute decisions about things like jewelry, perfume, and how much cash to take with you.

Your date pulls up to your house, and your first impression about this man past your initial interactions is based on the type of car he drives. You deem the car practical and attractive and give it a stamp of approval. You enter the car and it smells and looks clean, another couple of points in his favor.

At the restaurant, he does everything you expected in terms of being a gentleman, pulling out your chair and complimenting your dress. But now it's time for the real test. It's time for a conversation.

Before, when you'd first met, you'd been walking through campus at university. He is in one of your classes and you'd had a few short conversations about the class before he asked you out. You have yet to have a real conversation that doesn't feel like small talk, and you are nervous. You wonder, is her nervous too?

So, this is a pretty typical scene, I think. How are you going to navigate the conversation to figure out more about this man's personality and inner workings? You may think of keeping the conversation in pleasant, safe territory for a while at first, like hobbies and personal interests, career goals, what he likes about his classes, etc. This will offer some general overview information about what he is passionate about and to what degree. Just as in the interview setting, a person can gauge just how interested or passionate someone is about a given topic by the way the person answers the questions and how much effort goes into those answers. If someone has to think very hard to think of something he/she is passionate about, it might mean that this person has literally no interests and spends his time surfing the internet aimlessly or something. A lot of people prefer that their partners have at least one pastime that they really care about because it demonstrates some capacity for passion and excitement. These are fun, sharable qualities that extend to other parts of one's life.

This general territory is also a good place to start if you want to know a little more about a person's financial situation and goals. Someone who doesn't give a lot of thought to money might mindlessly mention how he's run up his credit card recently, then laugh about it as if it is not a big deal and even funny. This might be a good indicator that he/she is lazy and careless when it comes to financial issues; a poor quality in a partner for sure. If the person has clear goals for a career or occupation and seems to have a plan for how to get where he/she wants to go, this is an indicator that the person is not careless about money, at least in the long-term and care about laying out a plan to make his/her future possible.

Let's go back to Shaina's date and assume that they've moved past these general conversation topics. What can Shaina do or say to probe further into this man's personality and character without coming off like an interrogation officer? There are a few tricks you can use, and these will apply to situations outside the dating world as well.

If you really want to dig deep and feel confident you can pull it off, this trick will reveal a lot about the person you're interacting with. This will only work appropriately if the person is a genuine acquaintance and not someone who knows you well. If the person knows you pretty well already, your behavior might be obvious or simply confusing.

Now, think about what you don't want to see in a person. If you are looking for a romantic partner and are confident in your skills, think about a facet of people that you do not like. Your task now is to make a small gesture or comment that aligns with the type of person you want to avoid and see how this person reacts. Let's look at an example from Shaina's perspective.

Shaina looks around and notices a couple at a nearby table. They are also dressed nice for the restaurant, but Shaina wants to gauge whether or not her date is a snob. So, she says nonchalantly, "wow, did you see that couple over there? How did they get in?" Now it's time to observe.

Does he look over? What does he say in response? Does he agree or look confused? Has he been noticing other people as well or is he completely focus on you? Keep in mind that this is a strategy that is most appropriate when you need to sum up a person quickly and are on the fence about whether or not you want to invest more time getting to know this person. Throwing out inconspicuous comments and phrases are a useful tool for quickly gauging a personality without investing hours and hours of time. Let's look at another example.

Shina receives her plate of food and the server says he will be back shortly to make sure everything is satisfactory. Shaina takes a bite of her food. It is delicious, but she's going to perform a little experiment. She makes a comment like, "Oh my god, this is terrible. Should I have them take it back?" Now she listens to his response.

Depending on his response, Shaina can collect some interesting details about the deals with certain kinds of situations, and we will look more deeply into how to evaluate responses in the next chapter. For now, Shaina is downloading the information she is receiving from this man's behavior and responses. Does he seem reserved and unassertive toward the situation with the server and Shaina's food? Or does he jump to her defense and assure her that she should say something. Or perhaps he jumps in himself when the server returns and assumes control of the situation, not allowing Shaina to get a word in while he explains that her plate of food is terrible. Does his frustration rise to a level far beyond Shaina's in the first place? All of these responses are valuable data, and Shaina may base her decision regarding future dates on this information.

The difficulty in getting to know new people is that there is a variable amount of time in which a person may maintain a façade which simply reflects the best version of themselves, or else what they presume another person wants to see. People experience this all the time in romantic situations in which two people find a spark and date for a few weeks before their "true" personalities start to show themselves. Using probing questions and experimental comments to observe a person's reaction and behavior in response is a way to essentially catch the person off guard and force him or her to resort to their natural tendencies in response to an unexpected situation or comment.

Now that Shaina has conducted her experiments, we will look at how to evaluate and read into a person's responses in this and similar situations, both verbal and nonverbal. In some cases, experiments like these may come in handy to bring out whether someone interacting with you is consciously being deceptive. In the next chapter, we will look at a variety of contexts for the application of this strategy and discuss how to evaluate and apply that evaluation to categorize people based on the big 5 personality categories as discussed earlier in this book. I would also mention that if you conduct an experiment like this and are pleased with the outcome, you should tell your partner about the experiment to foster honesty if you decide to turn this acquaintance into a relationship. Constant trickery past the dating phase is not exactly a valued characteristic!

UNDERSTANDING AND REPLYING TO THE MESSAGE

WHEN USING A STRATEGY LIKE ASKING PROBING QUESTIONS and throwing out comments to gauge reactions, it is important to pay attention to everything that is going on within the responder's actions. It is also important to have an idea of what you are looking for and why before attempting to probe a person in this way. Think about the questions, "What exactly do you want to know about this person?" "What would you consider a poor response in these situations?"

To illustrate, let's return to our example of Shaina on her date. She'd just met this man on campus after a class they'd had together. She decided she was interested in learning more about him, but she's wasted a lot of time in the past on guys who turned out differently after a few weeks of getting to know them. This time, she's decided to conduct her own experiments to bring out any potentially unattractive or undesirable character traits hidden underneath.

When she and her date are out to dinner, she experiments by

seeing if she can draw out some kind of snobbish comment by making a comment about a couple sitting nearby. Let's look at a couple of different reactions and what you can read in each case.

Shaina says, "wow, look at that couple over there. How did they get in?"

Assuming this is an upscale restaurant and people are required to dress up, this comment may lead to a number of different reactions from her date. He may respond with something like, "oh my gosh, yeah, I agree. He looks like he just rolled out of bed. Is that shirt from Target?"

Well, now we've got some information.

Part of your evaluation in a situation like this might center around whether or not there was a visible shift between the person's demeanor a moment before and their demeanor after the comment is introduced. The comment above suggests that this person may be a bit of a snob. At least, this is one interpretation you could glean from the comment. This person could also simply be jumping at the chance to align themselves with Shaina in order to gain favor or rapport. He sees it as a way in, and Shaina now has some deliberation to do.

The body language will also tell Shaina about her date personality. If he raises his eyebrow and rolls his eyes, it may suggest to her that he truly feels what he is saying because he is displaying a genuine reaction, though this can be faked. If he uses gestures and enthusiastic body gestures, this also indicates someone who may be quite a people pleaser when it comes to dating women. Who really feels that strongly about other people eating in a restaurant? Let's address the other experimental comment before evaluating personality type possibilities.

Shaina receives her food and decides to throw out another situation to evaluate her date's response. She makes a comment about how her plate of food is terrible, perhaps she directly asks him what he thinks she should do. His response could be one of several reactions. Perhaps he responds quietly with a gesture that equates to "keep your voice down." He says something like, "No, no, don't do that. Not here. I'll take you somewhere else afterwards."

So what does a comment and gesture like this mean? Shaina may interpret this reaction as a sign that he can be quite demure and unassertive in situations where he is afraid of being embarrassed or sticking out. He may be overly concerned with appearances and genuinely afraid of calling attention to himself because he hates the feeling of being embarrassed. This reflects a variety of possible personality traits.

Let's evaluate both of these responses according to the big 5 categories to see what we can glean from this small pool of information.

To review, the big 5 personality categories we discussed earlier are openness, conscientiousness, agreeableness, extraversion, and neuroticism.

How would you evaluate the first response in the dating scenario? His willingness to readily agree with Shaina may demonstrate a genuine distaste for people who don't spend as much money on appearances or a genuine interest in simply aligning himself with Shaina to gain rapport. The first response may reflect a high degree of self-centeredness and judgment which may fall in the category of extraversion. There is a high level of self-awareness in terms of comparing one's self to others and casting judgment freely. Shaina's date physical gestures heighten this response and lean towards a more snobby, arrogant side to his personality. This may also be interpreted as a degree of neuroticism in his intense awareness of physical appearance, and his response to another's appearance reflects a concern for his own appearance that may be too high to be reasonable. On the other hand, there is a level of conscientious behavior in the second response demonstrated by his automatic alignment with another for whom he feels attraction. He places things in an order that he feels will gain him favor and this response reflects a desire for "correctness." Saying something contrary to Shaina's verbal judgment would feel incorrect to him since his aim in this endeavor is to get Shaina to like him more.

In response to Shaina's second experiment, let's say Shaina's date responds demurely, telling her he will take her somewhere different afterwards and that she should stay quiet about her food. Shaina's date seems to portray another set of personality traits. He seems very concerned with how a complaint at such a fancy restaurant would reflect on his personality. Which of the big 5 categories reflects this kind of attitude and how would you evaluate such a response in terms of each?

In this example, the level of openness can be interpreted in a variety of ways. On one hand, he seems vulnerable in his willingness to contradict Shaina and reveal how he truly feels about the situation. He is revealing here that he has a true, distinct fear of embarrassment and is essentially asking Shaina not to do anything that would make him feel this way. His fear at this moment overrides any air of arrogance which had previously been displayed through his response to the first experiment. He is also displaying a high degree of conscientiousness in his conviction that they must play by the rules of etiquette in this setting, careful not to upset the status quo or cause an upset. Tied in with this may be the possibility of some neuroticism going on connected to his anxiety about embarrassment and readiness to discard his façade in order to protect himself.

It is difficult to pinpoint exactly where this man lies on all of these scales, but these evaluations provide a broad starting point for Shaina to determine his dominant personality type and traits.

Let's move to a different arena and see how experimental probing and phrasing can help you determine personality and traits in another context.

You are a male business executive at a business function at which you are expected to mingle and meet people who are higher up on the ladder than you. You are invested in this company and are committed to developing a rapport with those who may help you as you climb the ladder yourself. You only have one evening in which to make a lasting impression, and you also want to gauge what these people are really like. Who are they really? What do they really think of their company and employees and mission statement?

You begin by introducing yourself as the few familiar faces bring you around to those they know. Finally, you find yourself settled with a drink in the corner and a couple of guys who seem to get along with your personality and sense of humor well. They are the picture of where you want to be in a few years, and you decide you should tap into this resource as soon as possible before the night is over or they lose interest in you. How do you read them in terms of how they feel about you? What do they think of the company and the likelihood that you can achieve what you want within it?

One strategy is to begin by inciting some form of gossip. You phrase a comment like, "Oh, I didn't notice him when I came in, the one frowning in the corner over there." This is an open-ended comment that may or may not encourage further discussion. Either the men know the person and have some details to share, or they don't know the person and the conversation must move on. There are things to pay attention to the outside of just what these men are saying. You pay attention to their body posture and gestures. What are their faces telling you? Are they displaying signs of boredom or deception? A lot can be gleaned from taking note of the eyes. Remember how genuine smiles are said to "reach the eyes." Pay attention to whether or not these men are genuinely smiling or just pretending to enjoy your company. They may be preoccupied with other thoughts and concerns or they may be growing bored. Shift topics until you receive a sign that one or both of the men you are talking is interested in something you just said. Remember, one of the most efficient ways to gain rapport with an acquaintance is to talk about them and make them the center of the conversation. Listen to their answers and repeat some of the exact words they've just said to you back to them as you progress. People love to hear that you're paying attention to them and that you are interested in talking about their life or opinions. If you are having trouble engaging topics regarding the information you want, start by building a sense of trust by asking questions about the person's life and goals. How has working at this company brought them closer to their goals?

When you've developed a connection, you will see physical signs to reinforce that connection. Look at the orientation of their torsos and their feet. Are they pointing more directly toward you in these respects? More so than when you first began talking? If so, then this is a good sign. Leaning in to one or both of these individuals while you talk will also help pull them into your orbit as you circle in closer to the topics you want to broach.

It is now time to throw out some experimental comments to gauge their reactions. You make a comment such as, "At my old job, my boss used to talk about some of the new hires behind their backs." The comment is chosen based on something you want to discover about your own boss or the boss you would have once you move up and are promoted, the one these two gentlemen currently work under. If you have concerns about the boss's personality or ethics, gage their reactions as you mention these concerns in conjunction with an old boss or someone you used to work with. The men's reactions, both verbal and nonverbal, should provide some information regarding their boss.

If they see resemblances between the character of your old boss or coworker and their own boss here, depending on the level of rapport you've developed in the short time frame, they may choose to release details to you. They may lean in closer and roll their eyes or move their eyes around as if to make sure the person they are talking about is nowhere nearby. This is a good sign for you. You've developed enough of a connection and sense of trust that you are now winning your desired information. Alternatively, the men may clam up in response to your comment if what you are talking about sounds familiar and they are not yet willing to reveal information about their boss to someone they've only just met. This is also a good source of information because it tells you that they have at least recognized some of the content you've mentioned and are associating this information with their own superiors.

Finally, if the men's response is completely flat and reactionary, it may signal to you that what you are saying is not a familiar trait that they associate with their coworkers or boss, and you can breathe a little easier in this respect.

Identifying Deception

Finally, you may want to keep in mind the tools you can use to figure out if someone who approaches you is trying to deceive you for some reasons or another. The key to uncovering a deceptive acquaintance is similar to some of the strategies criminal investigators use to determine if the suspect is lying to them during an interview. As always, pay attention to body language that signals that they are creating a story rather than recalling an experience or telling the truth about themselves. We will dive deeper into body language in chapter 10, but some of the simplest signs of deception occur when they fumble on answers in response to complex or direct questioning. Ask them to repeat the information they say several times while they are talking to you and see if they have trouble recalling their exact words or exact details. Interrupt them to see how well they can reorient themselves and respond to a question about something they said earlier. If they clearly recall a series of events, they should be able to conjure the details quickly. Inject words and gestures of agreement to strengthen their own confidence. Does the story or detail become more elaborate? Does their affect change to suggest they are happy to be winning you over? These may well be signs of deception. Look over-exaggerated gestures and fumbling of details as well as fidgety behavior and lack of eye contact. All of these may point to a likelihood of deception, and you should remove yourself from the situation.

In the next chapter, we will examine more thoroughly the principles and characteristics of human connection, an experience which is essential to every human being's mental health and happiness. Connection is a powerful starting point for influence and is essential to a relationship in which each receives the benefits of happiness and banishing loneliness.

MAJOR COMPONENTS OF CONNECTIVITY

HUMAN CONNECTION AND THE MAJOR COMPONENTS THAT are involved in human connection are vital for learning and understanding a person's personality and how it was shaped. Personality traits are large determined through genetics but are also shaped by experiences in a person's life. Most people hold on to secrets regarding their pasts because of negative emotions associated them, such as anxiety, fear, and sadness.

Before we move on to a deeper discussion of reading people through body language and other cues during an interaction, I wanted to discuss why a lot of the strategies utilized to gain people's trust or build rapport actually work. Why does a person tend to like me better when I use their name in conversation or repeat the things that they say to let them know I'm listening to them? When does a person's body orientation tell me about how they feel about me in general? Why does someone willingly go along with a group decision when they really don't personally agree? These behaviors are intimately connected with both personality and societal rules and pressure. Let's first examine how each of the big 5 personality categories forms connections in conjunction with their associated personality traits and characteristics.

As discussed previously, different big 5 personality traits influence human interaction in different ways, both positively and negatively.

The first personality trait we will examine is openness. You can probably guess already that someone who is high in openness is going to have a much easier time connecting with others, and you are right. The personality dominated by openness describes someone who is waiting and willing to connect. Many factors may go into this mindset, and it doesn't mean someone is in a perfect mood all the time and wanting to talk to people all day. But openness presupposes a natural curiosity and interest in others. People who are open genuinely want to make connections because it feeds a source of joy for them. It connects nicely with traits found in the extraversion category, in which a high degree of extraversion means that a person receives a lot of energy just from interacting with other people.

These traits can be apparent within seconds of interacting with someone who is high in openness and extraversion. Sometimes without even realizing it, this person is a master when it comes to the principle that you get what you put into it. Through letting people talk and listening to their words, an open person naturally forms a bond of trust, especially if they are willing to show themselves in terms of their vulnerabilities.

Nothing brings two people closer together than going through a challenging experience together or opening up about a challenging past that has shaped you in some way. Most people are afraid to open and let others see where they are vulnerable because they are afraid of adverse reactions. When you form a bond of trust with another person, this fear tends to drop away as you unload more and more of what challenges you emotionally in your life. This is why a person with a high level of openness can form such incredibly strong bonds and friendships. Their friends know that they've seen this person in an honest way and that they can trust them with their own feelings of vulnerability.

Agreeableness goes hand-in-hand with openness and involves even more interpersonal strengths. Connection with others is facilitated by the natural tendency to want to please and respond to other people, even those who are not so high in agreeableness or openness. They tend to be more positive in their outlook and perspective toward other people and more readily see the good things about people rather than the not-so-good.

Someone who is high in the other traits, conscientiousness, and neuroticism, might be a little tougher to reach in terms of making connections. The traits inherent in these personality types involve a natural guardedness that must be addressed before trying to engage in a more personal relationship. Though this may be the case, the strategies for reaching people like is not so different from the general rules of gaining someone's trust and building rapport. The focus should be on showing your own vulnerability as a way to encourage them to feel comfortable revealing more about themselves. You shouldn't expect someone to drop their guard if you are unwilling to meet them halfway in order to show that you are someone who can be trusted. Be genuine and honest about yourself and listen to the words the person responds with. There may be a great deal of emotional pain dominating their thoughts and behavior patterns. These can be seen through physical cues and body language in addition to the words being spoken. Remember that it is important not to intimidate and scare away guarded individuals if you are trying to develop a relationship with them, either working or romantic or otherwise. Do not approach straight on, as we discussed earlier, but approach from the sides and orient yourself to face in the same direction. This works as a subtle, nonverbal cue that you are not here to hurt them but are there to help and learn from them in some way.

State your intentions soon after the interaction begins and provide reasoning and rationalization for why this person should stick around and converse with you. Perhaps you share an interest. This is a great way to begin a conversation with someone who tends to be guarded because it opens up an avenue that bypasses the small talk that introverts are usually turned off by. Make a comment that relates to the common interest and see how the person responds. Remember that a bad interaction may have nothing to do with you. It may just be a bad time with something going in their life that they do not wish to share with others.

Alternatively, make a connection with them by mentioning that you know someone who is close to them, a friend or family member. Creating ties of trust will help you appear more trustworthy because someone they know has approved of you. This may help you get the ball rolling in terms of a productive interaction. Remember that the general rules of social interactions apply, even to those who are more introverted and reserved. People love to hear their own words repeated back to them, and they love to hear people use their names. Utilize these strategies consistently, and you will see the barriers slowly start to break down.

Connection and Influence

In today's modern world, intimate human connection has become more difficult to experience organically because everyone seems to be hiding behind a wall of cold, stoic technology. Social media offers the appearance of social connection, but communication with other people through these means doesn't come near to what it feels like to have a human being sitting next to you and looking into your eyes as you exchange words. There is simply nothing electronic that can replace that experience. We've invented ways to make such interactions possible at long distances through things like Skype and FaceTime, but these are still poor replacements for real human interaction. Superficial human connections are encouraged through social media like a giant popularity contest, and most of the time what you are seeing on people's social media profiles are lies and facades that only reflect what people want others to see. You see your old friend from high school on a vacation somewhere exotic at an expensive resort and you think, wow, she's got it together! But all you're seeing is the pretty face of a much more complex entity. We all do it, we all want to appear put-together and in high social standing. That's why programs like Facebook became so popular in the first place. Marketing has certainly caught on, and now it is pretty much impossible to do anything on social media without behind inundated with targeted ad campaigns. This represents one sphere of what we will call the "connection and influence" phenomenon which contrasts with the in-person, one-on-one experience of connection and influence. How are they different, and how are they the same?

Online and social media marketing is focused on targeting desires and getting people to click on ads that lead to enticing offers for things that the person has expressed interest in, like clothes or tools or experiences. This data-driven connection leads to influence in the realm of personal desires and wants and appeals to our sense that we need things to make our lives better. Marketers have gotten very good at exploiting strategies like time-sensitive sales and creating urgency by expressing they only have a limited number of items available, etc. But goods marketers aren't the only ones trying to grab your attention. We also have "influencers" vying for attention and being paid to wear certain brands or use certain products in order to reach a wider audience. These influencers have gradually taken over the space where celebrities like music artists and Hollywood actors and actresses had once held. Now we have an endless number of niche markets and personalities who are congregating around certain people, brands, and products, and the number of available niche groups and social circles to get into continues to grow exponentially as new ones are constantly being created. Something as simple as a few YouTube videos and a Twitter account can be enough to launch an internet sensation and create a following of people based on your personality. This sphere of influence is attractive because it feels immediate and creates the illusion that you are in the company of thousands or millions of other followers who are just like you or at least have similar personalities and senses of humor. You can feel this need being quenched as you scroll through live feeds and comments as someone is speaking on YouTube or Facebook live stream. Gamers latch on to their favorite e-sports heroes and watch their videos while commenting on gameplay with friends. Gaming itself has become a worldwide method for social contact that has taken the place of in-person contact, sometimes to a staggering extent, in many people's lives. Over time, lack of real interpersonal connection manifests itself as loneliness and depression, and we can see actually happening reflected in research. As technology and social media take the place of real human contact and interaction, we see people isolating themselves and living in solitude, losing social skills and cultivating fear and anxiety around actually having to interact with people with their own voices.

Within this context, having the skills to reach and connect with other people organically and without a phone is becoming a valuable and rare skill set to have. Connection and influence in the sphere of in-person interaction is a powerful experience for anyone, but especially young people in today's world. The challenge is to be able to grab someone's attention and hold it through real personal interaction that feels real as opposed to the superficial social media experience many of us are used to. But when this does happen, the experience is memorable and satisfies a craving deep inside all of us that works as a soothing balm to treat the isolation-based loneliness people have inadvertently cultivated in their own lives. If you can make powerful connections like this, the potential for your power of influence becomes endless.

Let's illustrate this happening through an example in which a man successfully approaches a woman in a public setting, resulting in an interaction and conversation that prompts the woman to put aside her phone for the evening.

If we imagine a public place, like a piano bar, in which everyone has come on their own, you might imagine the scene resembling the same one you see standing in line at the checkout counter or at the airport—every single person is looking down at their phones. Many are playing games, and many are texting or surfing the internet or checking their Facebook feeds, etc. And a lot of the time, sadly, even when people are together in groups socializing and having a good time at a bar, half of them are spending more time looking at their phones than interacting with their friends.

Let's imagine there is a young woman at the bar alone with her phone in her hand. It's important to note that a lot of people use their phones as a way to hide their anxiety and fears of being conspicuous. The approach is important, and the man must also pay attention to the body language that follows in order to know how to proceed further. As we've discussed and will discuss in further detail in the following chapter, body language tends to say a lot more about what a person is thinking than anything that comes out of their mouth. The goal is to approach on a human level without intimidation. Making your approach loudly and conspicuously will only embarrass the woman. Quietly interact, ask questions, and focus the conversation around the woman will help develop an interest. Other factors, like physical attraction, will certainly come into play and are outside of the man's control. But a lot of times, men with average looks can make up for it by displaying genuine interest, honesty, and vulnerability in conversation. If the man in our story is heading in the right direction, he will notice physical cues, like the woman turning her body more toward the man. As the conversation progresses, the man will know if she is interested if he can successfully hold her interest to the point where she stops looking at her phone. If this happens, you know that not only is she potentially interested in the man as a person, but he's also successfully made her feel comfortable enough that she doesn't feel the need to hide behind the phone.

Let's discuss how the subtle art of body language, cues and redirection can lead to an opening for connection in as little as a few seconds.

EXAMINING OVERALL BODY LANGUAGE, CUES, AND EXERCISING REDIRECTION

The vast majority of communication we receive from other human beings is nonverbal. Professionals train for a year to recognize subtle body movements, gestures and facial expressions that tell them what those people are really thinking and if it is consistent with what they are saying. Let's move further into a discussion of body language and how to evaluate a person's thoughts from them.

Body language, in general, is simply an outward expression of what a person is feeling in the moment. It can be prepared, such as for a speech, but the words are prepared in this scenario as well, so this is why it is difficult to tell much about a person's true personality and intentions through a public speech.

. . .

But when you observe a person speaking to others in a place and setting where they are allowed to act naturally with people they know, you can pinpoint how someone is feeling simply by observing their body language from across the room. You don't even have to know what they are saying to pick up on these signals. You can discern things like temperament, demeanor, intention, and authority. Let's begin with the body language of authority and domination.

Authority and Domination

This is a good place to start because a lot of what I'm about to point out to you will feel intuitive, though there may be things that you hadn't specifically noticed for much of your life. These signals are right before you all the time, yet they work subconsciously to influence and persuade under the radar.

In America and other Western countries, it is customary to give and receive a handshake when you are meeting another person for the first time. The scenario can be casual, like a friend introducing you to another friend in a restaurant, or it can be a business affair, where you are meeting a potential business partner for the first time. In both of these situations and many in between, it will feel quite natural to offer your hand as well as a smile. So what does the handshake tell us about another person?

The first thing to notice when you are given a handshake is the pressure of the shake itself. Does it feel like the person is shaking your hand with equal pressure to your own? Or does it feel like they are trying to crush you like the Hulk? Is the handshake weak and limp, almost falling out of your hand? All of these handshake styles will tell you something specific about the person shaking your hand, including how they feel about you.

The handshake of someone who views him/herself as being in a dominant position will tend to exert more pressure in the handshake and twist the hand so that it is over top of the opposition's hand. You may recognize the ancient Roman expression of having "the upper hand." The Romans used to shake hands in a similar way but inverted so that the thumbs interlock and arms form Vs in opposition to each other. Whoever ended up with the dominant position in the handshake was given additional benefits after a battle and was first in line to receive food and wine.

You can see an example of this expression of domination in the televised meetings between President Trump and Canadian Prime Minister Justin Trudeau. President Trump tends to exert strong force in his handshakes as well as assume the dominant position of placing his hand over top.

When you shake someone's hand who asserts a position of authority through this gesture, the feeling goes right to your gut. You get the feeling that this person is going to tell you what to do and you will follow. Even if you're not thinking these specific thoughts in your mind, you subconsciously submit to the authority in front of you. Therefore, if you yourself are trying to exert confidence and/or authority in a situation, remember the power in a handshake.

In public speaking, there are also behaviors and body language that works effectively to communicate specific feelings about you in the audience. We all tend to use our arms and hands when we are speaking as a way to further our expression of the words we use. You can tell when someone is really into telling his/her story when the arms and hands are flying around everywhere, trying to demonstrate visually what the listeners weren't there to see at the time. Similarly, someone who is speaking in front of a large audience with the intention of getting people to like them, or "buy" them, will use hand gestures and use their bodies to help them communicate and project his/her convictions outward. In this situation, it is very important for the speaker to pay attention to the positioning of the hands.

Gestures with the arms that involve down-facing palms are a clear signal to the audience that this person is authoritative in some way. The audience may feel that they are receiving instruction and commands rather than receiving a message of persuasion. Some people respond positively to a demonstration of authority like this, but downward-facing palms may trigger a defensive reaction in listeners if this person has not yet won them over. This is why someone speaking to large audiences as a fairly new figure should pay attention to their hand position. Speaking with upward-facing palms is a sign of openness and agreeableness, to reference our big 5 personality traits. Upward-facing palms suggest that the person is kind, agreeable, and inviting the audience gently into their arms as a gesture of peace and goodwill. Even if the speaker's intentions are far from goodwill, this simple hand placement communicates this message to the audience subconsciously. Upward-facing palms suggests to the listener, "I have nothing to hide," and "I want to join with you, hear me out," etc. When an audience receives a speech or a sales pitch or anything where the speaker is gesturing with hands facing up, they will tend to feel like you are approaching them on equal footing and not trying to assume control from them. It is a non-threatening form of nonverbal communication.

Let's examine the opposite extreme. A speaker who is gesturing not only with down-ward facing palms but also using the pointer finger to accent his/her words is signaling to the audience something like, "you better do as I say." This feels like a command, and you can do a little experiment yourself. Have someone you know give you a direction using each of the three hand gestures. First, have them ask you to do something with their hands facing upward as they gesture, may walking you through the steps to complete the task. Take note of how this makes you feel.

Next, have your friend give you the same direction with their hands facing downward as they map out the steps in the task. Take note of how this makes you feel, also. Lastly, have them point at you and point out the steps with their pointer finger during their directions. Take note of what feelings this conjures in your gut and review.

. . .

You probably had the strongest adverse reaction to someone pointing their fingers at you and using their pointer finger to explain a task to you. This is because pointing fingers is a very strong signal of asserting dominance and authority. If a speaker has not yet won over an audience but is assuming this gesture, many people in the audience are going to automatically get defensive, even if they don't recognize it consciously. They will be harder to win over and to be convinced of the speaker's propositions, even if they are good ideas!

This is why body language is so important. Body language communicates things and evokes emotions that many people do not even pick up on as it's happening. It's kind of like subliminal mind control. When something says that they "have a bad feeling" about something, it's usually because they've received some unconscious signals that tell them to be cautious, even if the warning is not accurate in its assertion. Similar to someone with an anxiety disorder, it is possible for the body to interpret something or someone as threatening based on subtle signals, even if there is no actual threat.

Confidence

This is a big one. Many people go to conferences, buy self-help books and listen to motivational speakers talk about the subject of building and growing self-confidence. What many people are surprised to learn is that the way that you choose to hold your body in space has a huge influence on how you feel. Consistent practice focusing on your body posture and how you hold yourself in public will have a drastic effect on your self-confidence.

Here's an experiment used by speaker David Snyder. Stand up, wherever you are reading this, and think of a time when you accomplished something extraordinary. Maybe it was something you weren't sure you could do, but you pulled through. Remember how amazing it felt to accomplish such a task and how you felt right afterward. Now, holding that memory in your mind, raise both of your arms over your head in a giant V pose with your hands made into fists; think Rocky. Now, hold that pose.

After holding that pose for a few seconds, thinking of your major accomplishment, observe how you feel. Do you feel good? Better than you did a few seconds ago? Good. Now, let's try to flip the experiment.

While holding this posture of victory, try your hardest to feel bad. That's right, try to make yourself feel less confident or sad about something. Hard to do, isn't it?

The way we hold ourselves in space has a lot of influence over our feelings of confidence. Let's try one more. Sit back down where you were sitting and reading and slump your shoulders forward. Make yourself small in your seat with the worst posture you can conjure. Think about a time when you failed to accomplish something you really wanted to accomplish. Now, how do you feel? Hold this position for a few seconds. You may feel a weight returning to your shoulders and your mood suddenly dropping a few ticks. That's because your body is suggesting to your subconscious mind that all is not right in the world. Now, holding this posture, try to conjure the feeling you just experienced when you were standing with your arms upraised in a victory pose. Hard to do?

Assuming certain gestures and postures will influence your emotions, sometimes even more powerfully than thought alone. This is why many motivational speakers will encourage listeners to practice smiling and good posture, even if they don't yet feel like doing those things. What listeners find is that simply by forcing themselves to smile for a few seconds, their mood automatically lifts from where it was a few seconds ago when he/she was frowning. The same is true for posture and confidence. If you have an important presentation coming up and are a little scared, practice holding yourself up straight, shoulders back. Keep your chin lifted, even when you are feeling scared. With consistent practice, you will start to feel more confident automatically. Practice this around the office and wherever you are in public. You will start to feel that fear gently lifting over time.

So, how does this apply in the dating scene? Imagine you are at a party and there is a young woman in the corner. She is attractive, but she is also slumped over and staring at her phone. She doesn't look very happy. What the woman might not realize is that her posture is sending very specific signals around the room. She may be open to a conversation, maybe even looking to start a relationship, but her posture suggests to the other people in the room that she does not want to be approached.

. . .

A person who wants to be approached in a public setting may find the following information about human psychology very useful.

Human beings are hard-wired to value status. Therefore, in a public setting where you want to be approached by someone new, you might think about going with some friends and being the center of attention. Orient your party at the center of the room or club or bar and start talking to everyone. Tell them a story. When people see you in the middle of a group of people who are paying attention to you, it signals that you are someone they should try to get close to, if simply out of a desire to raise their own personal status. Once this happens, all kinds of doors open up to you. As many people in the dating world soon realize, the hardest part about it is the initial approach and the first few minutes of an interaction.

When you've learned to recognize and embody the power of body language, you can open up new avenues of control that most people remain completely unconscious of during the interaction. Exude confidence and happiness, even when you don't feel it initially, and soon, those feelings will come. It is an incredible phenomenon, and one with an endless array of possibilities to work in people's lives. You may have heard the phrase, "fake it 'till you make it." Well, in this case, it absolutely works!

. . .

In our final chapter, we will review the wonder of being able to analyze demeanor, mood, personality, and confidence level through the various strategies and principles outlined in this book. We will also take a look at one final strategy for reading people; the ancient practice of Chinese face reading. Though this practice has been around for a very long time, many people in the Western world have not heard of it. You will be amazed as we dig into how you can simply look at an adult's face and discover things about their pasts. Applying this people reading strategy in a variety of settings will give you an additional tool for influence and building trust.

THE WONDER OF SUCCESSFULLY ANALYZING OTHERS

Now that we approach the end of this book, hopefully, you have a much more full understanding of how being able to read others can be utilized in daily life in a wide variety of settings and situations.

A lot of what we've talked about in this book has dealt with reading gestures, body language and other gestures from a relative distance. In this chapter, we will close with perhaps the most personal and up-close strategy for reading other people. That is, Chinese face reading.

This practice works under the assumption that what appears on a person's face and how that face is constructed betrays what is going on inside their minds and inside their bodies. There is so much about a person you can glean from a person's face that there are years of observation and research that we will only briefly touch on in this chapter. I'd like to focus in on just a few of these observations that will be most pertinent in your goal of reading people very quickly. Most people and casual acquaintances are not going to be open to you staring at their faces for long periods of time, so let's discover a few things that you will be able to see instantly when you look at another person's face.

Every adult human being has lines and wrinkles on their faces as a result of a lifetime full of what is called "micro-expressions." Microexpressions are an outward expression of an internal emotion. For example, we generally associate a person whose mouth is downturned at the corners with someone who is sad. It is something we see and recognize instantly because it is universal. Similarly, when we see someone whose eyes disappear into a smile, we associate that with a genuinely happy person who expresses genuine happiness on her face. Over time, expressions of emotions on our faces form lines that are distinguishable and identifiable.

For example, the lines that appear just over the eyebrows on the outside are associated with being skeptical, and the Chinese refer to these lines as skeptic lines in the practice of fade reading. A person with pronounced lines in this area is someone who is very skeptical and requires a lot of evidence to be convinced of an idea or proposition, etc. As a speaker or businessperson, when you meet someone with lots of defined lines in this area, you know you are going to have your work cut out for you!

Traveling outward and going back to the person who laughs a lot, the lines at the outer corners of the eyes that move upward signify joy. Someone with defined lines in this area has spent a lot of time laughing and smiling genuinely. These lines will also tend to signify someone who is high in agreeableness, and perhaps openness and extraversion as well.

On the opposite side, if you see a person who has defined lines at the outer corners of the eyes that arch downward, this signifies sadness. A person with defined lines in this area has experienced a great deal of sadness and may have spent a considerable amount of his cumulative life experiencing grief or depression. Lines that extend even further down toward the cheek express a deeper and deeper level of this prolonged experience of sadness.

Moving toward the center of the face, there are lines that will tell you a lot about the person's purpose in life and how committed he/she is to that purpose.

If you see lines which extend from the outer nostrils toward the corners of the mouth, these are the purpose lines as defined in Chinese face reading. Someone with these lines has had an experience that led to a commitment to a specific purpose or life goal. He/she is probably very committed to whatever this goal is. If you see these lines on an acquaintance, a good conversation starter might be asking about his/her passion in life. There is a high probability that their eyes will light up at the chance to tell someone else all about it.

There is another area where you can a signifier that a person has experienced personal transformation in some way, shape or form. This line appears on the forehead and stretched from the inner corner of the eyebrow up toward the hairline. If you see this line, it may signify a powerful experience that has happened in the person's life which has led to great personal changes. Again, a great way to gain rapport with a person like this would be to ask questions and give this person the opportunity to share more about his/her great experience.

Moving inward, you may see lines in the very center between the eyebrows. This is a quite common set of lines and signifies that someone is irritated or annoyed or impatient. You can imagine the expression on someone's face who is impatient, perhaps stuck in traffic or in line at the bank. Their eyes are annoyed and there is a definite crinkle in between their eyebrows. Someone with lines in this area spends a lot of time making this expression and probably harbors a much lower tolerance for annoying and impeding situations than others. You may see people from time to time whose lines in this area are so defined that it seemed they are permanently frowning. If you see meet someone with defined impatience lines, you should be wary of trying to convince them or talk their ears off when it comes to something you are trying to sell, whether it is a product or an idea.

If you move to the center of the face to the bridge of the nose, there is a possibility that you will see lines extending outward from the mid-portion of the nose. These lines are defined as being lines of disempowerment. What this means is that the person is a big people-pleaser. Perhaps the person would score so high in agreeableness that he/she has fallen victim to the tendency to try to please everyone because there is a fear of how a person will react if he/she fails them. This is a visible reflection of the fear that is harbored deep inside. You may see these lines on highly neurotic people as well if there are strong feelings of fear in conjunction with other people's reactions to them. Perhaps they had a very disempowering experience in their childhood or young adulthood where they tried to stand up for themselves and received such a harsh pushback that they continue to run away from that feeling well into adulthood. In this situation, it will be very important to tread lightly and avoid physical signals of domination or intimidation because they will be very sensitive to it. When talking to someone with disempowerment lines plainly visible on her face, try to adjust your tone and gestures to be as open, honest and non-intimidating as possible. You will need to work a little harder in a situation like this to convince someone that you mean no harm.

These people may be a little harder to reach than someone who is highly agreeable with clear joy lines on their faces. Now you have an idea of how powerful being able to read a person's face like this can be when you have certain intentions and need a plan of action to reach different kinds of people. The more you experiment and practice on people, the more positive reactions you will receive as people are amazing at how natural perceptive you seem to be.

Combining People-Reading Skills

You will find that once you've mastered the basics of people-reading strategies, including analyzing personality type, cold reading, body language, and how to respond in kind, you will be able to reach people on a wider scale and create avenues of influence specific to your personal goals. Whether it's dating and finding a romantic partner or becoming a high-powered business executive, these skills will translate to whatever it is you aim for in terms of social standing and influence. Remember that a lot of these skills happen on a subconscious level, and a lot of the time people will never even know you are utilizing this knowledge to essentially decode them. Let's look at a scenario in which you might be able to use many tools at once to paint a picture of a person before you've even finished the first conversation.

Going back to singles at a bar, you see that young lady we discussed earlier who is sitting alone in the corner with her nose buried in her phone. She is attractive, so it seems strange that she is all alone. Though most people will take this as a sign that she does not want to be approached, you may decide that there is something going on, and you decide to investigate.

As you approach, she looks up. What is the expression on her face? Does her posture shift? What do the lines on her face tell you about her current emotional state?

Before you begin to analyze, the fact that she's looked up at all is a big win. You've accomplished this feat by approaching from the side, not straight on, which can be interpreted as intimidating. When she looked up, you were careful to express a genuine smile that reaches your eyes and you give her a slight nod. You're not too overbearing with your gestures, but you are careful to remain open and friendly.

As she looks up, you notice that she is returning the grin that you offered, and she begins to sit up a little straighter. This is a good sign.

You move closer and orient yourself to face the same direction as the young woman, perhaps asking if you can take the seat next to her. At no point have you approached straight on, you are conveying an air of friendliness and express no intention of intimidation. She says yes, that's fine. You sit.

Her posture has improved a bit, and when she looks at you, you see that she has very defined joy lines at the corner of her eyes. But she also has skeptical lines which are very defined as well. What does this mean for you?

The joy lines may indicate that she is ready and willing to listen to you say something funny to make her laugh. She appreciates humor and spends a lot of time laughing and enjoying her time with other people. The lines indicating skepticism simply means that she may be more careful than usual when it comes to meeting strangers, so the fact that you've managed to sit next to her and receive positive signals indicates a strong success so far in the interaction.

You notice that her body is more oriented toward you, so you initiate a conversation in which you ask questions about her life, though you're careful not to ask anything too personal. You notice that she has a trademark line on her forehead indicating some kind of personal transformation, so you decide to figure out what her passion in life is. She quickly responds to this and tells you all about how she's begun an organization whose mission she feels very strongly about. Perhaps she turns her chair a bit to face more directly towards you, and her feet follow this orientation.

The conversation is going well, and you decide to throw out an experimental phrase to gage her personality and general perspective on other people. You notice a couple walking through the door dressed in unconventional clothing and color assortment and make a gesture toward them with your head, "Look at them. What do you think?" This is a pretty straightforward and unmasked experimental phrase, but it will prompt some kind of comment from the young woman. She says something like, "That's interesting. They look like a fun couple."

Her response indicates that she may be highly agreeable as well as open. She is not quick to judge just because someone looks different from the norm.

At this point, you may feel that you've developed a sense of trust and good enough rapport to ask directly why she is alone. She replies that she is simply shy and waiting for her friends to arrive. She doesn't feel confident enough in herself to approach people on her own, so she decided to sit to the side and wait for her friends before talking to anyone. You remember that before, she had been sitting almost as if trying consciously to make herself as strong as possible. This conforms to the body language of shyness, not to mention that she has been making steady, positive eye contact with you as she speaks, indicating that she is not being deceptive.

You smile in response and express that you understand. Perhaps you describe some kind of vulnerability of your own to commiserate with her in this regard and build an even stronger bond of trust. At this point, the man is well on his way to a first date!

If this seems like an overwhelming amount of information, don't worry. The more you practice one skill at a time, the more you will see how natural it is to incorporate these strategies in your daily life. Once you make the connection between body and mind, making a habit of noticing people's body gestures and language in conjunction with how they express themselves, the conclusions you draw from your interactions with people will feel automatic and natural. Practicing and utilizing many strategies at once will only work to strengthen the confidence you have in yourself to read people and really get inside their heads. If you are intent on building yourself up within a community, whether at work, at school, or at home with family, all of the strategies will help you get there once you learn to truly observe and pay attention to what is going on. Consider a daily mental focus practice such as meditation in order to strengthen your presence of mind. If you are constantly distracted by your phone or thoughts that are not in the present moment, you will find that it is very difficult to pick up on these small cues and signals from other people.

CONCLUSION

Thank you for making it through to the end of *The Art of Reading People: A Psychologist's Guide to Learning the Art of How to Analyze People Through Psychological Techniques, Body Language, and Personality Types*, let's hope it was informative and able to provide you with all of the tools you need to achieve your goals, whatever they may be.

The next step is to think carefully about how you are going to utilize these tools of people reading. What is it you are really curious about? What is it you want to accomplish with this knowledge?

If you are unsure, I suggest conducting a little writing/thought exercise. You will need a piece of paper and something write with. Alternatively, you can use an app on your phone or compose an email to yourself.

First of all, start by writing out your thoughts about how it feels to have the knowledge you need to begin reading people. Do you feel empowered? Does a specific goal come to mind? Write down whatever pops into your head.

Now, think about where you lack confidence in regard to how you personally portray yourself in public. Do you feel shy around people? Do you feel you might lack the confidence to go out and use these tools for reading people? Do you feel somewhat isolated socially and are looking for a way to connect with others?

Recall from an earlier chapter how we discussed the importance and necessity of human connection in every person's life. No one survives on their own in isolation. They would perish within a few hours or a few days of birth. We are hardwired to need and seek out a human connection in many different forms. If you look deep inside yourself and discover that you are indeed lonely, then it is time for you to make an effort for yourself and your health to go out and connect with others. With these people-reading tools, you should feel more empowered to approach the situation with strangers more confidently. Simply remember to breathe and observe. Don't get so caught up inside your own head, thinking only of what could go wrong, that you don't see the obvious signals coming your way from others. This is the power of connection. When someone realizes that you are truly paying attention to them and listening to what they say, you will develop an almost instant rapport and sense of trust, as we've discussed all the way through this book.

Also, practice the postures of confidence we talked about earlier. To conjure a source of power and confidence, practice assuming the victory pose and holding it. Pay attention to your posture in public. Don't get so caught up in what other people are doing that you forget your own signals you are projecting to those very people. Yes, it takes a pretty high level of focus, but as with any skill, you just need time and practice to develop a level of skill that makes it all look and feel effortless.

Don't forget the power of a genuine smile and genuine eye contact with others. That human connection begins with someone feeling safe around you. Don't stare at the ground or broadcast your fear and hesitation. Remember, fake it 'till you make it. Keep that eye contact and smile until you start to feel the confidence making its way into your body. Keep your posture tall and confident, even if it takes a few seconds for this posture to translate into a true feeling of confidence. Remember that most people are going to be receptive to openness, vulnerability, and honesty. Someone who is defensive may simply be looking for the first small sign of deception, so don't give it to them. Don't offer a free excuse for someone to write you off by averting your eye contact out of shyness or fear. Practice in front of a mirror if you are unsure how you are appearing to others when you approach and start a conversation.

If you are looking to make a statement in a room full of peers, exercise confidence with a dash of authority to gain people's respect and desire to pay attention to your words. Remember when you meet people that the first bit of information, they are going to receive from you comes from those few moments of physical contact that comes from a handshake. Keep your grip firm, but don't force the upper hand if it doesn't feel natural. Scaring people away or causing them to dislike you is not a very good start toward the art of persuasion. You may have some very good ideas you want very much to share with them, but if they don't buy you, then they won't be buying anything you have to say. Be strong and confident through your posture, but as you speak, keep your hands upturned so that you are displaying a non-threatening demeanor along with a sense of urgency and genuine conviction in your own words. You will see right away as people begin to draw toward you, listening intently to what you have to say. Be careful not to point at anyone in your circle as this will trigger a feeling of defensiveness and sometimes even anger toward you.

You may be inspired to watch some speeches given by famous speakers or leaders. Watch them and how they use hand gesture and facial expression to not only convey the emotion in what they are saying but also to draw an audience in and develop a sense of intimate trust, even in a crowd of thousands of people. Watch where they place their hands and where they choose to insert subtle gesture of power and dominance. Perhaps when the topic shifts to those over whom the speaker wants to exercise dominance, the tone shifts to reflect this persona of power and the gestures become more intentional, with palms turned downward.

Returning to your written exercise, take a moment to really think about your social goals and how you believe these tools are going to help you reach them. Visualize yourself in the scenario where you have successfully reached your goals. There is a whole world of research and practice surrounding the concept of positive thinking and visualizing one's goals consistently over time in order to make them happen. Return to your goals each day and put yourself back in that scenario in which you can see yourself clearly, having accomplished your biggest life goals. Your idea of success in this respect may encompass many different areas of your life. Perhaps you want to be a better partner by being to read how your partner is thinking and feeling. Or maybe you are that business professional looking to give yourself an edge over others to get to your dream job with your dream promotion. The idea of the thought exercise is to banish the tendency to think of these things as only dreams. Visualize yourself in a successful situation and create the mindset in your brain that you already own this outcome, that is yours for the taking.

Positive thinking reflects something called the "law of attraction," which you may already be familiar with. Many books have been published on the subject, and many profess to have experienced incredible things as they learned to put this law into practice every single day. If you are not keen on the idea of meditation, think instead of this thought exercise as a way to organize and focus your mind on your goals. People who do not have a clear goal in mind will have a lot more trouble accomplishing and getting to where they want to in life than those who draw a clear picture in their minds of what they want and who they want to be. Don't be afraid to see yourself in an extraordinary setting that once may have seemed far outside your reach. Just as the information in this book may have started out as overwhelming, all it takes is time and practice to make something arduous start to feel natural.

Finally, I wanted to impress upon each and every reader of this book just how important it is to own a sense of responsibility and discretion when it comes to using the tools and strategies for reading people in this book. It is a wonderful experience to learn how to read and understand people through strategies like face reading and understanding body language, but these tools are not meant to be used to manipulate people for fooling them for your own personal gain. It is one thing to successfully influence people and use strategies to make people more open to your ideas and suggestions, but outright using things strategies as a way to justify wrongdoing toward others in your mind is not the ethical way to be using these tools. Remember that there is a big difference between the practice of criminal profiling in law enforcement and criminal investigation and racial profiling that is prevalent in many areas of the United States. It is never ethical or accurate to associate crime with a specific race, gender, socioeconomic status, or other external factors. True criminal profiling is a product of hard facts and drawing conclusions based on established data.

If you've found these concepts helpful and fascinating, I would encourage you to explore even more the vast amount of research and knowledge available to you online through established professionals in their fields and their lectures and books. The more we learn to understand each other in terms of our commonalities, the more we can work together to build a more peaceful, just and understanding world community. All of us want to connect with others who are willing to set aside a little time and effort to listen and understand who we all are and what we are all trying to say to each other. This could be as simple as saying something like, "I understand" during a conversation with a complete stranger or saying thank you and making eye contact with people in the service industry as you grab your morning coffee in the morning. As we learned about the basic concepts of Chinese face reading, people micro expressions over time will be broadcast all over their faces as they grow older. Brightening someone's day through basic human connection brings us full circle from our beginning goals of social influence as we work to create a world in which people are more open and willing to accept human connection in everyday circumstances and scenarios. There is also a great deal of research to suggest that practicing basic human kindness and gestures of connection goes a long way towards improving overall health and wellbeing. Give yourself as many advantages as possible when you decide to move forward with your goals by fostering the attitude and demeanor that you hope to find in others all around you every day.

Finally, if you found this book useful in any way, a review on Amazon is always appreciated!

Lightning Source UK Ltd.
Milton Keynes UK
UKHW020700020120
356253UK00013B/907/P

9 781087 855226